THE SHADOW OF A DOUBT

CONFRONTING CHALLENGES TO FAITH

THE SHADOW OF A DOUBT

Confronting Challenges to Faith

Talbot Davis

THE SHADOW OF A DOUBT
CONFRONTING CHALLENGES TO FAITH

Library of Congress Cataloging-in-Publication Data

CIP Data has been requested.

15 16 17 18 19 20 21 22 23 24—10 9 8 7 6 5 4 3 2 1
MANUFACTURED IN THE UNITED STATES OF AMERICA

CONTENTS

INTRODUCTION

Shadows of Doubt

They wake me up at night.

Sometimes out of the deepest kinds of sleep.

And once they wake me up, it's awfully hard to pick up where I left off.

What am I talking about? Bumps in the night? Sounds in the house?

Nope. Doubts in my head.

I have doubts about this thing that I claim as the center of both my identity and my vocation: the Christian faith.

And the doubts that wake me up from my slumber while rocking me to the core deal with the most pivotal issues of the faith:

Is God there?

Is God real?

Is God great?

Is God good?

What happens to the everlasting souls of people who die without ever hearing of Jesus?

Is the Bible reliable?

Why did John just have to tell us that he beat Peter in the footrace to the tomb on the first Easter?

Why do pomegranates do double duty as aphrodisiacs in the Song of Songs?

Am I selling people a false remedy to their very real problems?

I suspect that I'm not the only one to be assaulted with these questions of faith. Most people of faith will admit that they have doubts if they are being honest with themselves. In fact, your own doubts are probably the reason you picked up this book in the first place.

This wrestling is nothing new. I was not raised "in church," as they say, but I nevertheless had a dramatic encounter with Christ when I was seventeen years old. Yet not long after that conversion, questions like the ones I've asked above started to seep in.

A year later, I found myself in college—and in the kind of intellectual environment that celebrated doubt and ridiculed faith. So my doubts intensified. I remember picking up a then-classic book in the evangelical world, *In Two Minds: The Dilemma of Doubt and How to Resolve It,* by Os Guiness. The book made me feel better simply because I persevered and read it all—even though I was unable to grasp much of what it had to say. I was grateful for a book that expressed my faith mixed with doubt. The title resonated with me because I lived the title.

Fast-forward a quarter century and half a lifetime. In the course of pastoring at Good Shepherd United Methodist Church in Charlotte, North Carolina, what have I discovered? That people today—even people of great faith—are plagued with the same kinds of doubt that have been with me from the beginning of my belief. The people of this congregation honor me by bringing into my office their honest, raw, conflicted doubts about their Savior. Like the anguished father in Mark 9:24, they often cry out, "I have faith; help my lack of faith!"

So what do I do with the doubts of the people, both as their pastor and their fellow pilgrim?

It seems to me that people have long had these three kinds of responses to doubt:

1. Ignore them. If you pretend like the doubt doesn't really exist, pretty soon it won't. Focus on what you do know of the faith; pay precious little attention to what you don't know; and in the end, your faith in Christ will be like it was before. Unless it's not.

2. Explain them away. This is the approach many of us take when we treat that Bible as if it were a book—which it's not—and not as a library—which it is. When we misunderstand the nature of the biblical revelation, we are tempted to create all kinds of false harmonies in between its texts. In contrast, I believe that the highest view of the inspiration of Scripture takes into account that the books of the Bible are often in conversation with one another. They even, at times, correct each other. If you doubt me on that, read the Book of Proverbs. Then read Ecclesiastes. There is some serious conversation and disagreement between the two authors who wrote those books.

3. Cave in to them. All too often, people respond to their very real doubts about faith by taking the easiest route of them all: They abandon faith altogether. The weight of doubt piles up; the lure of life without restraint seeps in; and the next thing you know, a follower of Jesus suddenly is not.

As you might imagine, I don't find any of those solutions to doubt's dilemma very satisfactory. So, along with the people of Good Shepherd, I came up with a very different approach to the doubt of faith:

What if instead of hiding in the shadow of our doubt, we were to bring our doubts into the light?

Instead of ignoring them, explaining them away, or caving in to them, I believe that we should take our doubts and expose them to the light, fearlessly acknowledging them and wrestling with them in the open. We should be honest about doubts, unafraid to acknowledge them and shine the light of Christ on them. When we do so, are we not likely to discover that a faith that has gone through its shadows of doubt and then emerged on the other side is, in fact, a faith worth having?

I believe it is. That conviction stands behind the chapters, activities, and conversation guides in the rest of this book. Because I believe that when we dig deep into our doubts and excavate them with a community of faith, we rob them of their power and we strengthen our faith.

And who knows? Maybe they'll stop waking us up in the middle of the night as we rest with assurance that Jesus is Lord and there is no other.

Talbot Davis

1

BELIEVE IT AND NOT

"I have faith; help my lack of faith!" (Mark 9:24)

I conducted a little experiment in getting ready for this series called *The Shadow of a Doubt*. I anticipated the series so much that as I prepared for it, I did something I've never done before: I took an online poll. On the Good Shepherd Church Facebook page, I posted a simple question about faith and doubt and asked people to respond. I asked the online community, which includes both Christians and non-Christians, "What is the source of your doubts? When it comes to your faith, what doubts do you bring to the table?" This open-ended, two-part question invited people to share any and all doubts they had about God, or Jesus, or the church, or heaven and hell, or themselves, or anything else that might relate to their faith. I knew that I would get a lot of responses, and I did. Here are some of the answers I received:

> *Whenever a young life is taken, or stolen, especially in a violent manner, I always ask, "Why?" If everything on earth belongs to God, including the children, why does he allow those things to happen?*

I get to the point where I feel helpless . . . there are so many poor and suffering people . . . I feel like we aren't making a dent.

I doubted my faith and his love when I lost my best friend to cancer.

Wonder why some babies are born with deficiencies when they haven't had a chance yet and the mother did all the right things during pregnancy.

Sometimes when prayer goes unanswered or the outcome is bad I doubt if praying makes a difference.

I don't think there's room on Facebook for all mine. . . .

Some of those doubts may be your doubts; you might even feel like that last person, the one whose doubts would fill Facebook. And the answers that came in privately, which I can't share, were even more painful and poignant than the ones printed above.

IN THE GAP, THE SHADOW OF DOUBT MAKES ITS HOME.

But the reason I did that survey about doubt—and the reason I'm doing this series—is that I have them too. I have doubts. Doubts about God, and Jesus, and the Bible. I proclaim a gospel of faith, and I too live in doubt's shadow. Is God real, or am I perpetuating some kind of heavenly pyramid scheme on the poor people of Good Shepherd? And if God does exist, is God real *for me*? If I can struggle through that first doubt to believe that God exists and all those smart atheists are wrong, what's it like to believe God exists for me? Is the God *out there* at all concerned or involved with my life? There are other doubts, too: What happens to the souls of people who've never heard of Jesus? Why did blood have to be shed for sins to be forgiven? Why did God allow acne and male pattern baldness? I have important and trivial doubts about all sorts of things related to my Christian faith.

I'm willing to bet that I'm not the only one who has ever considered these and other issues and, through it all, wondered if it wouldn't just be easier to stop believing. I don't care what that song by Journey ("Don't Stop Believin'") says, sometimes I think that if I can just stop believing, it would make things better. It's hard to live in tension, where the faith I have and the faith I want to have are not the same. There's this faith and confidence we all wish we had, and then there's the faith that we actually do have. There's a gap between the two—sometimes spanning a great distance—and in that gap, the shadow of doubt makes its home.

In that gap is where the father we find in Mark 9 makes his home as well. As we will see, he is surrounded by the shadow of doubt. This is one of my favorite stories in Scripture, and it has one of the greatest lines the whole Bible. We'll get to that line shortly; but to fully grasp its power, we have to read the whole story leading up to it. The account of this father with a demon-possessed son takes place in Mark 9:14-29:

> 14 When Jesus, Peter, James, and John approached
> the other disciples, they saw a large crowd surrounding
> them and legal experts arguing with them. 15 Suddenly the
> whole crowd caught sight of Jesus. They ran to greet him,
> overcome with excitement. 16 Jesus asked them, "What are
> you arguing about?"
>
> 17 Someone from the crowd responded, "Teacher, I
> brought my son to you, since he has a spirit that doesn't
> allow him to speak. 18 Wherever it overpowers him, it
> throws him into a fit. He foams at the mouth, grinds his
> teeth, and stiffens up. So I spoke to your disciples to see if
> they could throw it out, but they couldn't."

19 Jesus answered them, "You faithless generation, how
long will I be with you? How long will I put up with you?
Bring him to me."
20 They brought him. When the spirit saw Jesus, it
immediately threw the boy into a fit. He fell on the ground
and rolled around, foaming at the mouth. 21 Jesus asked his
father, "How long has this been going on?"
He said, "Since he was a child. 22 It has often thrown
him into a fire or into water trying to kill him. If you can do
anything, help us! Show us compassion!"
23 Jesus said to him, "'If you can do anything'? All things
are possible for the one who has faith."
24 At that the boy's father cried out, "I have faith; help
my lack of faith!"
25 Noticing that the crowd had surged together, Jesus
spoke harshly to the unclean spirit, "Mute and deaf spirit,
I command you to come out of him and never enter him
again." 26 After screaming and shaking the boy horribly, the
spirit came out. The boy seemed to be dead; in fact, several
people said that he had died. 27 But Jesus took his hand,
lifted him up, and he arose.
28 After Jesus went into a house, his disciples asked him
privately, "Why couldn't we throw this spirit out?"
29 Jesus answered, "Throwing this kind of spirit out
requires prayer."

Look at how it starts in 9:14-15: "When Jesus, Peter, James, and John approached the other disciples. . . ." Peter, James, and John have been with Jesus. These are some of the more well-known disciples, something like Jesus' own inner circle. You might think of them as the "A-Team" among the disciples. These three disciples have just been on top of a mountain with Jesus, as we read earlier in Mark 9:2-13. And while they were on this mountain, they saw Jesus become *transfigured*. That's the language church folk use to describe what happened to Jesus on the mountain, in front of Peter, James, and John. Another word for it is *transformed*. It was as if he turned inside out, revealing his true, inner self to his most trusted disciples. When he did, Jesus' inner self appeared as a brilliant, blinding light, with his clothes becoming purely, radiantly white. Through this and a series of other events on the mountain top, Jesus demonstrates to the awestruck Peter, James, and John that he is not godly; he is God. There is a difference. Jesus is not holy; he is *holiness itself*. He does not have light; he *is* light. He is not godly; he is *God*. At Good Shepherd, we sing a song ("Jesus, Only Jesus") that says, "You stand alone, and I stand amazed." That is what happens on the mountain as Peter, James, and John witness Jesus transfigured to reveal his true glory. As they descend from that literal mountaintop, a crowd at the bottom of the mountain rushes to greet Jesus, "overcome with excitement" (9:15). It appears that some of that radiant glory still rests on Jesus.

THE LIFE-GIVER VERSUS THE LIFE-STEALER.

As Jesus and his A-Team disciples, Peter, James, and John, come down from the mountain, he finds the rest of his followers arguing (verse 14). The B-Team disciples (what else would you call the group that includes Judas?) are surrounded by a crowd and caught in an argument with legal experts. While Peter, James, and John went up on the mountain for a holy light show, the rest of the disciples stayed back and had gotten themselves into a religious fight.

In verses 17-18, someone from the crowd steps out and tells Jesus the source of the argument: "Teacher, I brought my son to you, since he has a spirit that doesn't allow him to speak. Whenever it overpowers him, it throws him into a fit. He foams at the mouth, grinds his teeth, and stiffens up. So I spoke to your disciples to see if they could throw it out, but they couldn't." Notice all the violent verbs in that description of the demon and the boy: *overpowers, throws, foams, grinds*. The author of Mark knows exactly what he is doing here. With this vivid, violent imagery, he consciously sets up an incredible conflict between the force of light and life and the forces of darkness and death. Jesus has just been revealed as the light- and life-giver up on the mountain, and he comes down to a violent encounter with the forces of darkness. The verbs Mark uses clue us in to it, depicting the demon as a life-stealing force. It even tries to kill the boy directly through water or fire (verse 22). And this boy, the man's son, has been the victim of all that violence. It sounds to modern ears like epilepsy or something similar, but the man and the crowd—and the author of Mark—attribute it to demonic powers. Whatever it is, we know that it stems from a life-stealing force at work. Mark creates a battleground between the radiant Jesus and the repugnant forces of sickness and violence.

For years, Dad has had a front-row seat to this violent battleground. The boy's father has witnessed his son's trauma "since he was a child" (verse 21), watching helplessly as seizure after seizure has ripped at the boy. Violent, body-crushing, soul-quenching seizures happen right before the father's very eyes. And that's where Dad's been living for a long time. Some of us know exactly what that's like. Some of us have experienced at least a little bit of what the father is going through. Some of you have felt the sheer powerlessness of watching a child suffer when there's nothing you can do to prevent it. A child, or a grandchild, or a friend's son or daughter has battled life-stealing illness for a long time, perhaps even from birth; and you have a front-row seat to the struggle. Others have watched a similar battle at the other end of life, seeing a spouse or a parent slowly but surely waste away. Even though it wasn't as violent as what we see in Mark 9, it was unmistakable and unstoppable. For many of us, this is a place we've lived. And the front-row seat to the forces stealing life from loved ones is surrounded by the shadow of doubt. This dad in Mark 9, in an act of great faith, brings his son to Jesus for healing. Except when he arrives, where's Jesus? On the mountain with the A-Team. So the B-Team attempts to heal the boy—with B-Team results (verse 18).

That's when Jesus, in one of his harshest statements anywhere in the Gospels, gives this rebuke: "You faithless generation, how long will I be with you? How long will I put up with you? Bring him to me" (verse 19). Jesus' frustration there is in part with his disciples, but it's also with the simple fact that his time left on earth is limited. He has the urgent task to bring his followers up to speed on who he is and what he is about, and to surround himself with companions who get it. And Jesus expresses frustration that even some of his twelve disciples seem unable to act in his name.

**I HAVE FAITH;
HELP MY LACK OF FAITH!**

In verse 20, they bring the boy to Jesus, as he commanded. And when they do, the demon throws the boy into a convulsion; and we encounter another round of violent verbs: *threw*, *fell*, *rolled*, *foaming*. Just as before, Mark's choice of words and imagery heightens the conflict between the kingdom of God and the demonic powers of the world. There is a battle raging between the life-giver and the life-stealer, and the poor father and son are stuck in the middle of the war zone. Father and son have been at ground zero for years. Again, some of you know what that's like. You've been there to witness children suffer or parents slowly slip away. And you know what those circumstances can do to your faith. Whether it's a violent battleground or a more subtle, ongoing struggle, these are the arenas where the shadows of doubt so easily dwell. It's no coincidence that so many responses to my Facebook poll recalled suffering—especially innocent suffering—as a source of doubt. You can sit right there with it. "If God is, why am I . . . ?" Or "If God is *good*, why are we . . . ?" Some are living among these shadows right now, and a lot of others have lived there before. I certainly have.

Then, in 9:22, the father meekly asks Jesus to help "if" he can: "If you can do anything, help us!" That sets Jesus off again to the point that what he says next *appears* to put a lot of power and authority in the father's own hands: "'If you can do anything'? All things are possible for the one who has faith" (verse 23). Now, if we take that verse out of context, it sounds as though Jesus is saying that the father needs to have more faith. It sounds as though Jesus is saying that his level of involvement depends on the father's belief: "Believe harder, pray longer, dig deeper, and all your dreams will come true!" If you only looked at that one verse, you could preach that and teach that. Except, that's not how the verse works in context; that's not how Jesus' statement reads within the rest of the story. Because Jesus' words to the man set up the father's response, which is the heart of the whole story. After hearing that "all things are possible for the one who has faith," the man cries out in verse 24: "I have faith; help my lack of faith!"

I love that response. *I have faith and I have no faith*. I believe and I don't. I trust and I don't. I'm with Jesus and I'm not—all at the same time. It's ambivalent, as if to say he's right-handed and left-handed, Democrat and Republican, Tea Party and progressive, Methodist and Baptist all at once. "I have faith; help my lack of faith!" The response is double-minded and ambiguous. It's so very human. It's so very real. It's so very me. Believe it . . . and not.

Remember where Dad is. He is in the vortex of a battle between the radiant and the repugnant, between the life-giver and life-stealer. And at the moment, the life-stealer is a lot more obvious, a lot more front and center. The father has had a front-row seat to this ongoing battle. What he's saying is: Jesus, I wish I were with you. Part of me really wants to be with you, to believe you and trust you; but I've gone through too much. There's been too much pain; and I'm not with you all the way, Jesus. And some of us are in that exact place right now. We know this dad. We've been this dad. *I believe in Jesus until I don't anymore. I know that God is good; I just don't know that God is good to me*. We believe. And not.

Which is why Jesus' response here is such a big deal. Now, he has just said in 9:23 that you have to *believe* to get everything, right? "All things are possible for the one who has faith." So by that rule, this believing and believing-not dad shouldn't get anything. Except, that's not how it goes. The man's doubts don't affect Jesus at all. Instead, Jesus heals the boy. He commands the unclean spirit to leave the child and to never return. And with a horrible convulsion that leaves the child looking dead, the spirit comes out. When Jesus lifts him up, the boy rises, healed and free (9:25-27). Jesus could have spoken harshly to the man who has faith but lacks faith. But instead, Jesus speaks harshly to the evil spirit (verse 25). The father isn't punished for lacking faith; he is rewarded for what little faith he has.

This whole scene is a battle for authority. Jesus stands in the middle of a battleground, and he takes this opportunity to assert his authority. It's radiant versus repugnant, life-giver versus life-stealer; and Jesus is the one in charge. He demonstrates his authority by ordering the spirit to leave, and it obeys him. And Jesus' authority goes beyond even that.

WHEN YOU ARE HONEST ABOUT WHERE YOU ARE, JESUS IS FAITHFUL TO SHOW WHO HE IS.

Mark includes the detail in verse 26 that the crowd thought that the boy was dead. But Jesus lifts him up alive (verse 27). Mark is no literary novice; his choice of words matters. By including this detail, he demonstrates that Jesus has authority even over death. Mark foreshadows the very resurrection of the dead in this act of healing. And it all comes about in spite of this father's lack of faith.

Remember, the dad is us. He is you and me, having faith and lacking faith at the same time. We've all been there. The father does not receive punishment for his doubts. He receives a blessing for his honesty about them. He believes it and not. And his son is healed. Here's what I take away from that: ***When you are honest about where you are, Jesus is faithful to show who he is.***

The father in this story is honest with Jesus. He's not evil or hostile, just authentic. He's had a hard time of it, and he's not going to pretend otherwise. He's not going to hide his doubt or try to dress it up. He's on the fence about Jesus and willing to put it out there. He wants to believe. He believes a little bit but somehow also doesn't believe at all. He's ambiguous, uncertain, doubtful. He might believe more under other circumstances, but he's seen too much. And he's honest: "I have faith; help my lack of faith." Something in that honesty, that real human tension between faith and doubt, resonates with Jesus. He takes the morsel of uncertain faith and blesses it. It's clear he prefers honest doubt over pretend faith. It's best to be honest with God about your struggles, whether they're a failing marriage or an addiction you can't shake or a sickness that won't go away. When you stop pretending and bring those real doubts to Jesus, he is faithful to come through and show you who he is. His own followers—the fighting B-Teamers—were doing a lot of pretending and not much truth telling. That's why the believing/unbelieving father gets the blessing and Jesus' disciples get the talking to. *When you're honest about where you are, Jesus is faithful to show who he is.*

If you've never doubted, you've only half-believed. Faith has never been easy, and doubts are not the enemy. Pretending is. If we've never doubted, never wrestled with issues of faith, our belief is about as deep as a puddle. But when we struggle through seasons of doubt, we emerge on the other side with a faith that is deep and tested.

THE CHOSEN ONES ARE THE ONES WHO WRESTLE.

It has always been this way. Think back to the Old Testament and God's chosen people. What's the name of the chosen people in the Bible? *Israel*. That name means "one who struggles with God" (see Genesis 32:22-32). The chosen ones are those who wrestle. The Lord loves the struggler and has no patience with the pretender. God is not intimidated by our doubts. God wants our honesty, our questions, our uncertainty. Jesus can handle all of it. He'd much rather we'd question him than ignore him. I'm not recommending this doubt as a place to live permanently; but if we find ourselves there from time to time, we don't need to be frightened. It's important for us to remember that salvation depends on the cross and not on our emotions. We are saved by the grace of God, not by what we feel. Even when we have doubts, we belong to Christ. If we are honest about where we are, Jesus is faithful to show who he is.

You know why I'm not frightened or daunted by seasons of doubt? Because no doubt ever diminished Jesus' authority. If you believe it and not, and if right now you're more "not," Jesus is still King. His level of involvement does not depend on your level of belief. Jesus didn't need the father's permission or confidence to heal the boy in Mark 9. He healed the child in spite of dad's unbelief. Mark highlights the father's uncertainty in order to elevate Jesus' authority. Jesus reigns no matter how much or how little we believe it. He really has that much authority over life. Over death. Over life after death. Believe it. And not.

Sometimes you'll hear church folk say that you can't question God. Really? Have you read the Bible? The writers of the Book of Psalms had some pretty tough questions for God:

How long will you forget me, LORD? Forever?
  How long will you hide your face from me?
How long will I be left to my own wits,
  agony filling my heart? Daily?
How long will my enemy keep defeating me? (Psalm 13:1-2)

No, God, it's because of you that we are getting killed every day—
  it's because of you that we are considered sheep ready for slaughter.
Wake up! Why are you sleeping, Lord?
  Get up! Don't reject us forever! (Psalm 44:22-23)

But I cry out to you, LORD!
  My prayer meets you first thing in the morning!
Why do you reject my very being, LORD?
  Why do you hide your face from me? (Psalm 88:13-14)

These were the writings of the Israelites, the chosen ones, the strugglers with God. God did not silence these questions; they became a part of our Scriptures. That's a powerful way to pray, a new level of honesty that comes from closeness and confidence in God. There is something in those raw, authentic questions, that refusal to pretend, that stirs up something in Jesus. It opens up a new pathway for God's power to be made known. God would much rather receive our ambivalent, true prayers of "I have faith; help my lack of faith!" than our fake "everything is perfect."

So can you? Will you? Will you be as honest with God as the guy who said to me in a text message, "I'm pretty disappointed with God right now?" Will you be as real as the sticky note out in the Good Shepherd lobby that says "I remembered God when I had to give my son back to him"? Imagine what it would be like if we were to have a church full of people who were so close to God they bring that unfiltered hurt to God. Imagine if we were to have a whole church of psalmists, who could ask God the really tough, personal, painful, doubtful questions. People who were willing to say: "This is where I am right now. But I'm going to keep bringing, keep praying, even keep trusting—until you show me who you are." Imagine if we were to have people willing boldly to stand before God in that place between doubt and belief.

When I conducted the Facebook poll on sources of doubt, I received one answer from a member named David Loy, of Good Shepherd. The response was a poem about the father in Mark 9, even though David didn't know that I'd be preaching on that passage for our first week of the series. Here is David's poem. I lift it up as an example of the raw, questioning faith I'm talking about, unafraid of doubt.

An Unbelieving Generation

Inside out
He stood on the mount
Two sides of the same coin
Belief and doubt
In the valley below
Spinning and flipping
And thrashing about
The convulsions of the boy
Transfiguring in my mind
The father of the boy—is me!
And I am he at the same time
Oh if I could only believe
I say it with my tongue
And before it is out
I am tossed about
In my own self doubt
"Help me overcome my unbelief"
Before it turns again—
To grief
It's not heads OR tails
I now understand
It's heads AND tails
That is part of the plan

To grow deeper in faith
By a doubting man
Not the actions of Him
But the reactions of me
Standing in the middle
Between doubt and belief
One side to fall
One side to stand
Getting stronger each time
I land on believe

Questions for Reflection and Discussion

Write responses and other thoughts in the space below each question. If you are discussing the book in a small group, prepare for the meeting by writing answers in advance.

1. What is the source of your doubt? In the space below and in conversation with your group, list some areas in which you sometimes doubt your faith.

2. Are you more likely to doubt that God exists, or to doubt that God exists for you and will help you? Explain your answer. What is the difference?

3. What is the most frightening aspect of the description of the boy with a demonic spirit in Mark 9? How would you have reacted had you been in the crowd?

4. What sorts of emotions or thoughts might the boy's father have experienced before he met Jesus? What about afterward?

5. The child's father both had faith and lacked faith (Mark 9:24). What was the source of his faith, and what caused him to lack faith?

6. Today are you more in the "believe" camp or the "not" camp? Why? How is this affecting your relationship with God?

7. Based on Jesus' response to the father, how do you think Jesus would react if you were to bring your raw, believe-it-and-not faith and doubt to him today?

8. This week's readings from the Book of Psalms contain some brutally honest words spoken to God. Have you ever felt familiar enough with God to ask those kinds of questions? If you have, what was the result? If not, what has kept you from asking them?

9. The message suggested that if you've never really doubted, you've never truly believed. How do you respond to that assertion? How have you experienced it in your life?

10. In the space below, write a prayer to Jesus, letting him know honestly where you are. How do you expect or hope Jesus to show who he is in these circumstances?

Pray Like a Psalmist

Read again through the words of Psalms 13, 44, and 88, printed on page 22. Choose one of the psalms and rewrite the verses in your own words, thinking about the struggles or doubts going on in your life or the life of your community right now. If you are studying the book with a discussion group, you may choose to divide the participants into three smaller groups and assign one psalm to each group. Or you may choose to have everyone work together on a single group psalm. In either case, be prepared to write the group version(s) on a chalkboard, whiteboard, or electronic display.

After you have finished rewriting the psalm, take a few moments to speak the new prayer out loud to God. Pray with confidence that God welcomes ours doubts and even anger. How do you hope God will respond to your prayer?

Closing Prayer

Lord Jesus, thank you that you are not offended by our doubts. Thank you that you bless our honesty and welcome our wrestling. In this prayer, I acknowledge that I struggle to believe and trust in the following area: ________________________________ (pause in silence to lift up the areas of doubt). I now wait for you to show up and demonstrate who you are. Amen.

Daily Scripture Readings

This week, read the following Scripture passages. As you read, recognize how the Scriptures invite us to bring our doubts to God with honesty.

Monday: Psalm 13:1-6
Tuesday: Psalm 44:1-26
Wednesday: Psalm 88:1-18
Thursday: Mark 9:2-13
Friday: Mark 9:14-29

2

WHAT'S THE ALTERNATIVE?

"Lord, where would we go? You have the words of eternal life." (John 6:68)

Note: The original version of this sermon was inspired by Andy Stanley's sermon "Consider the Options," delivered at North Point Community Church, Alpharetta, Georgia.

We like to have alternatives in life, don't we? It's true for most of us, if not all of us, that we like choices. If you were to go to a restaurant, for instance, and open the menu to find that the menu offered only one item, you probably wouldn't be happy. Even if that one item were something delicious like bacon, you'd still be disappointed at the lack of choices and likely wouldn't return to the restaurant. When you go to a car dealership, all of the different kinds of cars are laid out for you to compare. You can see the car you want in blue, gray, red, or even a different model. We like variety, the opportunity to find the thing that pleases us among many options. It's why a world like we see in the 2004 movie *The Stepford Wives* scares us. The women of Stepford are all supposedly perfect (as some people define it), but they are all suspiciously the same, and we know that something is badly wrong.

Our society is a choice-saturated culture. Twenty-first century America values choice as an integral part of its identity. Some of us can remember having only four television stations; now there are four *thousand,* and it's because we want our choices. If we don't like something, we like being able to opt out of it for something different. And this culture of multiple alternatives can help set the stage for a discussion about faith and doubt. If we doubt our Christian faith, we might wonder whether another worldview or way of life makes more sense or has things figured out in a better way. If we're bringing our shadows of doubt into the light, we can think about our faith and ask the honest question, "What's the alternative?" In John 6, we see Jesus' disciples consider that very question.

WHAT'S THE ALTERNATIVE?

Interestingly enough, John 6 contains a line that reveals Jesus' humanity in an especially poignant way. Usually when we think about the full humanity of Jesus, we point to another verse, John 11:35, the easiest Bible memory verse of them all: "Jesus wept" (NIV). You don't get much more human and emotive than that.

But a question Jesus asks in John 6 highlights his humanity in what to me is a more compelling manner, revealing even greater emotional depth and personal vulnerability than we see in his tears for Lazarus. We'll get to that question shortly. (Will you be patient with me here, please?) But first we need to recognize the background of the story. When we arrive on the scene of John 6, Jesus' popularity is dramatically on the rise.

Jesus does some things at the beginning of John 6 that radically boost his reputation. He's already got a "large crowd" coming out to follow him, because they have witnessed earlier healings and miracles (John 6:2). Then he feeds this large crowd of five thousand people miraculously with five loaves of bread and two fish (John 6:1-15). That sort of extraordinary, public event really got the people's attention. The people recognize it as a "miraculous sign," saying, "This is truly the prophet who is coming into the world" (John 6:14). Imagine how quickly the YouTube video of that event would've gone viral! Jesus receives a massive boost in his public perception as a result of this; in fact, he has to withdraw by himself afterward because the people want to make him their king (John 6:15). As if this isn't enough, Jesus walks on water later that night (John 6:16-21). Even though only the disciples witness that miracle, the crowd realizes that something unusual has happened when Jesus is gone the next day (John 6:22-25). They go looking for Jesus and find him on the other side of the Sea of Galilee. As a result of all this, Jesus' reputation among the people is growing rapidly.

Jesus uses the opportunity to teach some unexpectedly grand things about himself to the crowd he has gathered. He claims that he is the bread of life (John 6:35), stating that what God is doing in him is greater than the manna the Israelite ancestors ate in the wilderness. No doubt the boldness of that claim starts some grumbling in the crowd, the inevitable notion that "this guy's getting a little too sure of himself"; but it's nothing compared to what he says next. It's a speech that does a remarkably good job of killing his own buzz. Here it is, in John 6:53-69:

> [53] Jesus said to them, "I assure you, unless you eat the
> flesh of the Human One and drink his blood, you have no
> life in you. [54] Whoever eats my flesh and drinks my blood
> has eternal life, and I will raise them up at the last day. [55] My
> flesh is true food and my blood is true drink. [56] Whoever
> eats my flesh and drinks my blood remains in me and I in
> them. [57] As the living Father sent me, and I live because of
> the Father, so whoever eats me lives because of me. [58] This
> is the bread that came down from heaven. It isn't like the
> bread your ancestors ate, and then they died. Whoever eats

> this bread will live forever." 59 Jesus said these things while
> he was teaching in the synagogue in Capernaum.
>
> 60 Many of his disciples who heard this said, "This
> message is harsh. Who can hear it?"
>
> 61 Jesus knew that the disciples were grumbling about
> this and he said to them, "Does this offend you? 62 What
> if you were to see the Human One going up where he was
> before? 63 The Spirit is the one who gives life and the flesh
> doesn't help at all. The words I have spoken to you are spirit
> and life. 64 Yet some of you don't believe." Jesus knew from
> the beginning who wouldn't believe and the one who would
> betray him. 65 He said, "For this reason I said to you that
> none can come to me unless the Father enables them to
> do so." 66 At this, many of his disciples turned away and no
> longer accompanied him.
>
> 67 Jesus asked the Twelve, "Do you also want to leave?"
>
> 68 Simon Peter answered, "Lord, where would we go?
> You have the words of eternal life. 69 We believe and know
> that you are God's holy one."

Jesus' miracles have gathered and impressed a crowd, and Jesus has used the occasion to teach them about who he is and what he is up to. And just when the situation is pretty much perfect, just when he's on the rise and the sky is the limit, *Jesus keeps talking*. Things quickly take a turn for the odd and disturbing. What Jesus says is strange, shocking, perplexing: "I assure you, unless you eat the flesh of the Human One and drink his blood, you have no life in you" (verse 53). You know Jesus' handlers and PR folks were shaking their heads at that one, frantically gesturing to Jesus to just shut up before he made things worse. "Ixnay on the alkingtay, esusJay!" But Jesus keeps going, continuing to speak of eating his flesh and drinking his blood, seemingly oblivious to the offensive nature of it all. Jesus stops his own momentum with these odd, discordant words in John 6:53-59; and the disciples recognized it. The natural reaction would have been confusion and disgust. "Eat the flesh . . . "—that's cannibalism! "Drink his blood . . . "—that's vampire stuff! (Incidentally, the concept of Holy Communion is still a very difficult one to translate into cultures that are brand new to the Gospel, with no background knowledge of Christianity or Judaism.) At best, such words would have been confusing and off-putting. At worst, these are the words of a madman.

Perhaps the people thought that Jesus was using an unfortunate metaphor or symbol. Maybe they thought that he was off his medicines. Whatever it was, Jesus kills his own buzz. We know that much from the response in verse 60: "This message is harsh. Who can hear it?" The ones who say this are "many of his disciples"—his own followers. These are the ones who have been making him run out of bulletins every week. Now, all of a sudden, they're looking at one another and thinking, "I might not come back next time. I don't really like what I'm hearing." It starts what we might call an unholy murmur in the Jesus camp.

Jesus perceives this grumbling and asks in verse 61: "Does this offend you?" Eventually, it becomes clear that, yes, it does, in fact, offend many of his followers. As we read in verse 66—and can we acknowledge that we probably should expect nothing good to come from a chapter and verse numbered 6:66?—"At this, many of his disciples turned away and no longer accompanied him." The crowd hears these words, "eat my flesh" and "drink my blood" and everything else; and many of Jesus' followers decide that they are done because it's just too odd to follow.

When I read this scenario, I know something of what it's like for Jesus because it's happened to me before. He is going through every preacher's worst nightmare. I have made leadership decisions that have caused people to leave the church. I've had a demeanor or a position or a style that has caused others to leave. I have friends in ministry who have been decimated when people left in droves—on the level of half the church—in the wake of something they said or did. I can tell you from experience that having a John 6:66 moment shakes your convictions as a pastor and ruins your self-confidence. It makes me want to take up landscaping as my new career.

I don't know what kind of blow to his self-confidence Jesus endured as a result of his disciples' turning away in John 6:66, but I do know he asks a powerful question in verse 67 in response to this event. This is the question I told you about earlier—are you ready for it now? This question exposes Jesus' humanity and vulnerability even more than his weeping when Lazarus dies in John 11. Jesus has lost the crowd, some of whom had been following him as his disciples. The Twelve, his closest aides, might well be thinking along similar lines: "maybe we've been wrong to follow him." And in the wake of losing the crowd, Jesus addresses his core followers with his most painful, most human of questions: "Do you also want to leave?" Another way to translate this verse is, "You do not want to leave too, do you?" (NIV). He has lost the hundreds, so he turns to Peter and James and Bartholomew and the rest: *Not you too? Are you leaving me as well?*

I zero in on the question partly because I've asked it myself more than once. But even more than that, I resonate with this question because we are living in a John 6 world right now. The atmosphere of the twenty-first century United States parallels the situation in John 6 in more ways than I can count. It's a world where the words of Jesus and of Scripture on a wide variety of subjects seem so odd, so off-putting, so out of step with our culture and values, that people leave. The words of Jesus and the teachings of the Bible are so contrary to the conventional wisdom that people decide they are done. They leave church, leave the Bible, leave their faith. Think about all the words of Jesus and in Scripture that go against the grain of our American way of life. *Revenge*: Don't get it; don't seek it. Pray for those who wrong you. *The Self*: Self-control is a virtue in the Bible, and self-expression is not. *Sex*: one man, one woman, only in marriage, for a lifetime. *Money*: Give the first ten percent back to God instead of to your savings or a new iPad. At every level, from the private to the public, the Bible is every bit as offensive to our world today as "eat my flesh" and "drink my blood" was to Jesus' world then in John 6.

We live in a John 6 world, and studies and polls turn up some sobering statistics about the declining influence of the church in our society. Individuals and whole communities are turning away from Jesus, deciding they can no longer accompany him because of these confusing and off-putting teachings. And Jesus' question, "Do you also want to leave," becomes all the more haunting because it resonates in today's world just as loudly as it did in the first century. Jesus isn't just asking it of his twelve disciples back then. He is asking it of you and of me today. As people find more and more reasons to depart, Jesus wonders whether we also are going to leave. *Not you too? Are you leaving me as well?*

When you hear that question, the truth is often you're not quite sure how to answer it. Because, honestly, in the past or perhaps right now, your answer has been, "Well, I'm looking into it." I remember that religion class I took in college. The professor was so glib, so smart, so sure of his assertions that Paul didn't write the letters attributed to his name and that Jesus didn't say many of the words historically attributed to him. I was mesmerized by the professor's confidence and drawn in by his doubt. And toward the end of that semester, Jesus may well have been asking me, "Not you, too? You're not going to leave me as well are you?" I bet I'm not alone in having a class like that.

Or maybe today for you it's a different dilemma, such as depression that simply won't lift. The clouds hang heavy, the medications don't seem to be working, and you're sick and tired of feeling so sick and tired. Few phrases ring more hollow to you than the phrase "the joy of the Lord." So if Jesus were to ask you today, "Not you, too?" you might answer, "I'm thinking about it. What I've got isn't working."

Perhaps you're on the other end of the spectrum, and you have been really successful. You have the great job with the healthy paycheck, you've got the pretty girl and the obedient kids, you're in your early 40s and still have all your hair. You're getting all of that without Jesus' help, thank you very much. So what's the use? You've done just fine without Jesus, so why should you add him into your life now? Jesus' question to the disciples has become his question to you as well: *You're not going to leave too, are you?* This is a haunting question because I have seen people through the years answer in the affirmative: "Yes, I'm leaving faith." As Andy Stanley has said in a sermon on this passage, he has seen people walk away; make some of the most God-awful, life-destroying decisions; and then come back to faith five or ten years later. They still don't have their questions answered, don't have any of their doubts put to rest. They just have a debris field of wrecked relationships and ruined psyches in their wake. The most painful pastoral counseling I do deals with the aftermath of just those kinds of personal decisions and destructive seasons of life.

That is why Peter's answer to Jesus' question in 6:68 is pitch perfect: "Lord, where would we go? You have the words of eternal life." In response to Jesus' all-too-human question about whether his disciples were going to leave, Peter simply asks, "Where would we go?" Another way to translate the question is "To whom shall we go?" (NIV). In this simple question is a remarkable insight. If not Jesus, who else? Where else? How else? If we doubt, if we leave, Peter asks, *what's the alternative?* To whom will we go? Who else has the words of eternal life? Usually when we think about our doubts and our questions and our hesitations, we feel weighed down by them. But Peter turns it on its head and considers the other options. He thinks not only about the questions he has and the doubts that he harbors; he thinks about the alternatives and what implications they would have. Peter knows that if he were to leave Jesus, would have to go somewhere and follow something else, even if it's his own desires or plans. If he stops following Jesus, whom or what would he follow? If he stops believing Jesus, whom or what would he believe? If he leaves the community that Jesus has created, where will he go?

Have you thought about it that way? *If I stop Christ, faith, the church, or God, then where would I go? If stop this, then what? Where? How?* See, in discussing doubt we always wrestle with the questions; we rarely consider the alternatives to the beliefs we have. Is it nothing? That's tempting and freeing; it will make you feel as smart as Richard Dawkins or the late Christopher Hitchens. But it will likely lead to a descent into self-absorption; because, face it, your own desires and opinions then become the only standard by which your life makes sense and has purpose. You become your own god, and you will have the trauma of being in charge.

Or maybe another religion is the alternative? Is it like the woman who said to me years ago, "It doesn't matter really what religion you have, as long as you are a religious person"? That sounds like a nice thought. What about one of the religions of the East, such as Hinduism or Buddhism? Reincarnation is a key belief of theirs, and perhaps you wouldn't mind a second chance at this life. But in those systems, the ultimate goal of reincarnation is to get off the cycle and be absorbed into the universe. The goal is to become nothing. It might sound like an appealing system, but if nothingness—non-existence—is the goal then it is, in fact, deeply hopeless. Or what about Islam? Or Judaism? Of course, in both of those religions, eternal life in the world to come depends upon one's actions in this life. And can you ever be sure that you've done enough good or avoided enough evil to stand confidently before God when life is over? Christianity proclaims assurance of salvation because our eternal life depends on a Savior greater than we are. I can promise you that no religion is devoid of doubts, questions, and hard teachings that will make you want to turn away at some point.

JESUS ALONE HAS THE WORDS OF ETERNAL LIFE.

Another alternative might be something less specific, such as a "god of your understanding," to borrow a phrase from Alcoholics Anonymous. Such an alternative is non-judgmental, laissez-faire, and very tempting. It's the very thing Paul encountered in Athens while he was preaching the Gospel of Jesus Christ: "As I was walking through town and carefully observing your objects of worship, I even found an altar with this inscription: 'To an unknown God.' What you worship as unknown, I now proclaim to you" (Acts 17:23). Paul says to the Athenians that they worship a God whom they don't know, but Paul is now making God known in the person of

Jesus Christ. Our answer in the Christian faith today is the same as was Paul's on Mars Hill: Even in doubt, even with unresolved questions from really smart atheists, we have a name for the God of our understanding: Jesus Christ the Lord. Many people have come to Good Shepherd through recovery ministries and now rejoice that their higher power has taken on the name of the Highest Power.

When we consider the alternatives in the midst of doubt's shadow, we realize that Jesus alone has the words of eternal life. Jesus Christ is the eternal *Who* that towers over a sea of lesser *whats*. We will end up echoing with Peter: ***To whom shall we go?*** *Where else? What else? You're the only one with the words of eternal life!* Do you have a better idea? A stronger alternative? The answer every time is no. When you consider the alternatives closely, you realize that they stink. Jesus alone not only has the words of eternal life but is the very Word of God, the Way to eternal life. Don't just weigh yourself down with questions and doubts; weigh yourself down with the alternatives. Every other religious option, every other worldview or philosophy promotes some version of "Do this. Do that. Do more." Even atheism has its dos and don'ts, although they are groundless. Christianity alone says: "Done. Taken care of on the cross." What are Jesus' final words on the cross? "It is completed" (John 19:30). God does for us what we couldn't do for ourselves. It can't be earned, added to or improved upon. If you look at doubts that way, weighing the alternatives, you just might land with Peter: *To whom shall we go?*

Then Peter goes on in John 6:69: "We believe and know that you are God's holy one." Peter and the others have seen evidence of Jesus' power. They have witnessed who he is, and they know too much to go anywhere else. They've seen proof that Jesus has the words of eternal life; and because of that, they believe that Jesus is the holy one. And at some point, if you're a follower of Christ, you have experienced that, too. You and I have seen. Felt. Heard. Answered. I'm not telling you anything that you don't already know or haven't already experienced. If you're a follower of Jesus, you've experienced his power in your life before. I'm just reminding you of something that you may have forgotten when confronted by shadows of doubt and myriad lesser alternatives.

Sometimes when I hear Jesus asking, "Do you also want to leave," I confess that I'm tempted to answer, "Sorry, but yes." Sometimes my doubts cause me to look to alternatives and say that maybe following Jesus isn't for me after all. Whenever that happens, I remember my right shoulder. I played tennis in college, and I injured my shoulder during my senior year. The injury simply wouldn't heal, and even after four months of nothing but rest, it did not get any better. The doctor suggested surgery, which would have prevented me from playing my last season of tennis and ended everything prematurely. Of course, I didn't want to take that step if I could avoid it. So I asked a friend of mine who I knew prayed for healing to lay hands on me, to pray in tongues, and to seek healing for my shoulder. Julie, my wife, joined him in doing so. During those prayers, I felt the surge of divine electricity enter my body. It has now been more than thirty years, and I still haven't had that surgery. We have seen too much to go anywhere else. We believe and know that you, Jesus, are God's holy one.

I see further evidence that Jesus is God's holy one when I look at Good Shepherd Church. There are thirty-five different nations,

TO WHOM SHALL WE GO?

from every corner of the globe, represented on any given Sunday; it is a multi-generational, multi-cultural, multi-hued congregation. What we call *full color.* It makes no sense. There is nothing in my background that qualifies me to lead this kind of unique community. I'm a fifty-plus-year-old white man who grew up surrounded by people who looked exactly like me. I went to an Ivy League school. I played tennis, for crying out loud! But I am blessed to be a part of this incredibly diverse community of Christians at Good Shepherd. Nothing about it makes sense—but God. Where else would we go? Nowhere. Nothing else. Jesus alone has the words of eternal life.

I am not the only one who has witnessed God working too powerfully to deny. I know that others, too, have seen that Jesus has the words of eternal life, because they have told me so. A while back I received an e-mail from a mother at Good Shepherd, shortly after we had held an invitation for children to come to know Christ. She shared with me the following e-mail about her daughter, Kate:

> Kate was saved by grace on February 5th, 10 days before her 8th birthday.
>
> Because Kate has been spiritually fed from an early age, I often wondered if she would have an "ah-ha" moment. Her walk and faith have been so organic, like part of her DNA.
>
> Kate had a front row seat, from ages 2–5, to my mother's cancer battle and death. This experience profoundly changed all of us and created what I would call and "spiritual hunger" in Kate.
>
> Involving Kate in G-Force last year has revealed a true passion for God and given her a place to really blossom. Brian and I have said many times as this quiet, reserved girl sings and dances for hours in her room that the Holy Spirit was running rampant in our home.

> Our prayers were answered as Kate had a powerful encounter with the Holy Spirit on Sunday.
>
> She nearly dragged me to the car after service. While sitting in the parking lot, she said "I stood . . . I stood and I felt like I was going to cry so bad; I had to hold it in, Mommy. It felt good. I was happy but I had to cry!" The child who rarely cries had huge tears streaming down her face as she was most certainly moved by the Spirit. We talked about the Holy Spirit and how even though we can't see Him, we can feel God's love and power in our hearts when we follow Him and exercise our faith.
>
> She was unusually quiet all day. I could tell by her behavior and energy level that something transforming took place.
>
> She coveted the booklet you gave her and carefully filled out the questions on the back before tucking it in to a special box.
>
> Thank you for living by your mission of inviting all people into a living relationship with Jesus Christ . . . even the little ones.

For this mother, and for this pastor with whom she shared her experience, the work of the Holy Spirit in her daughter's life is living proof that Christ speaks the truth and our faith in him is well placed. It gives her confidence to say, with Peter, "You have the words of eternal life. We believe and know that you are God's holy one." *To whom shall we go?* We have seen too much to go anywhere else.

My guess is that the same is true for you. Time and time and time again you've seen Jesus' work and felt his presence too deeply for it to be anything but true. I'm not telling you anything you don't know; I'm simply reminding you of what we are all tempted to forget. You've tasted too much goodness and sweetness through the years, and so you know that the alternatives are nothing but empty promises. So many around us have decided that the Christian faith is not for them; and Jesus is asking you, "Do you also want to leave?" Before you do, ask yourself what Peter asked. "Where would we go?" Who is better, stronger, more liberating? *To whom shall we go?* I don't want you to be the one who walks away and then comes back ten years later without any more answers but with a debris field trailing behind you. Ask yourself in the midst of your doubts, "What's the alternative?" Jesus is not afraid for you to consider those other options, because God knows that you will see them for the empty promises they are. Jesus alone has the words of eternal life. Consider the alternatives; and when you do, I believe that you will come to celebrate that Jesus is the eternal *who* towering over all the pretend *whats*.

Questions for Reflection and Discussion

Write responses and other thoughts in the space below each question. If you are discussing the book in a small group, prepare for the meeting by writing answers in advance.

1. Do you like a restaurant with a long menu or a limited one? Why do you answer as you do? What about cars, clothing, television channels, music, and so forth? Do you prefer a lot of options or not many? What does this say about you? About the world we live in?

2. The message talked about how Jesus kills his own buzz while at the height of popularity. What specifically did Jesus say in John 6 to cause this reaction? How would you have responded to what he said?

3. Read John 6:61-65 closely. How do these words contribute to the reaction of the followers who turn away and leave in verse 66?

4. In John 6:67, Jesus asks his twelve disciples, "Do you also want to leave?" Do you think that he knew the answer that would come? How does your answer affect how you read the passage?

5. Have you ever driven away family, friends, or others who were close to you by words or actions that you felt were right? How did you respond to that situation? What gave you comfort or strength at that time?

6. What sayings or teachings of Jesus (or Scripture in general) do you find to be too harsh or bizarre? Which ones are most likely to make you want to leave? How do you make sense of these teachings?

7. Which of Jesus' teachings, or other parts of the Bible, are most against the grain of contemporary culture? Why is this the case? How should the church respond?

8. What comes to mind when you consider the question, "Where would we go?" What religion or worldview would you adopt were you not a Christian? How would this affect your life? What does this say about your relationship with Christ?

9. Both Peter and the message above remind us that we "have seen too much" of Christ's involvement in the world and in our lives to go anywhere else. Name some of the things you have seen that help you know that Jesus alone has "the words of eternal life."

Claim the Christian Faith

Close by reciting the Nicene Creed (pages 46–47), an ancient statement of the Christian faith that sums up the story and ministry of Jesus in all its glorious beauty. If you are in a discussion group, read the Creed out loud together. As you recite it, recognize that you choose to follow Jesus, God's holy one, rather than any lesser alternative.

The Nicene Creed

We believe in one God,
the Father, the Almighty,
maker of heaven and earth,
of all that is, seen and unseen.

We believe in one Lord, Jesus Christ,
the only Son of God,
eternally begotten of the Father,
God from God, Light from Light,
true God from true God
begotten, not made,
of one Being with the Father;
through him all things were made.
For us and for our salvation
he came down from heaven,
was incarnate of the Holy Spirit and the Virgin Mary
and became truly human.
For our sake he was crucified under Pontius Pilate;
he suffered death and was buried.
On the third day he rose again
in accordance with the Scriptures;
he ascended into heaven
and is seated at the right hand of the Father.
He will come again in glory
to judge the living and the dead,
and his kingdom will have no end.

We believe in the Holy Spirit, the Lord, the giver of life,
who proceeds from the Father and the Son,
who with the Father and the Son
is worshiped and glorified,
who has spoken through the prophets.
We believe in the one holy catholic and apostolic church.

We acknowledge one baptism
  for the forgiveness of sins.
We look for the resurrection of the dead,
  and the life of the world to come. Amen.

Closing Prayer

Lord Jesus, are you asking me that question? Are you wondering whether I'll leave you, too? Lord, although I've been tempted, I'm not joining with those who are leaving you. Looking at the alternatives shows me that you have the words of eternal life. Where else could I possibly go? Amen.

Daily Scripture Readings

This week, read the following Scripture passages. Think about how the true God compares with any alternatives and about what that means for your life.

Monday: Exodus 20:1-21
Tuesday: Acts 17:16-34
Wednesday: John 6:1-24
Thursday: John 6:25-71
Friday: Mark 8:27–9:1

3

NO LAUGHING MATTER

"Is anything too difficult for the Lord?" (Genesis 18:14)

"Yeah, right." You know what that phrase is, don't you? It's our way of responding to something we hear that we don't really believe. It's a mocking dismissal, dripping with sarcasm to write off something that sounds too good to be true. It's how we make it known that we don't have one bit of faith that what was promised will actually be delivered. "Yeah right" is something we say to laugh in the face of the chronic over-promisers and under-deliverers in our lives, a coping mechanism when we're confronted with those who stretch the truth. We're so accustomed to disappointment from some people or some situations that we've become cynical. We laugh, "yeah, right," at their latest claims or promises. I've done it; you've done it. I've said it; you've said it.

For instance, I'll see people out around town who haven't been to church in months; and they say, "I'll see ya Sunday, preacher!" And I'll say to myself, *yeah, right*. Or people from Good Shepherd Church will move to Mooresville—about fifty miles away—and promise that they'll still make the long drive down to Steele Creek for church every Sunday. As if there aren't any other churches in that fifty mile stretch—*yeah, right*. Of course, it applies to bigger issues than just running into your pastor at the store. We see politicians make claims that we know that they can't deliver. We read about a product that promises a cure for cancer, with no side effects, or a sure-fire prevention of hair loss. We hear someone say that next year the Panthers are going to win the Super Bowl. *Yeah, right*. Or maybe my favorite from the corporate world: We get an e-mail announcement at work that someone is leaving—suddenly and unexpectedly—to "pursue other interests" or to "spend time with family." *Yeah, right,* we think. We know what's really going on. We respond to all of these things with a collective *yeah, right*. It's an expression of doubt, our way of dismissing with a laugh the truth-stretchers, the over-promisers, and the under-deliverers.

**WE BELIEVE THAT GOD EXISTS.
WE JUST DOUBT
THAT GOD WILL SHOW UP.**

If we're honest, we must admit that we can bring this *yeah, right* attitude to our relationship with God. It is, after all, a form of doubt; and we've seen already that God wants us to be honest about our shadows of doubt, bringing them into the light rather than pretending they aren't there. There are times when we don't so much doubt God's *existence* as we do God's *involvement*. We can say that God exists, but we have a harder time saying that God is available to us and interested in our lives. Or we believe that God is great; we just aren't sure that God is good. We know the laws of nature, and we are familiar with the usual patterns of human behavior. We recognize the height of the obstacles we face in life, knowing that some of them are simply insurmountable. So when we see these grand promises in Scripture that everything will work out in spite of the obstacles we face, we respond to God in the same way we answer all of the other over-promisers and truth stretchers we've encountered: *Yeah, right*. As if to say, "You *could* do it, God; but I don't think that you *will*, because you usually *don't*."

When we bump up against those situations that seem intractable, the thought that God might rescue us, deliver us, and fix our problems moves us to sarcasm: *yeah, right*. We do this with big, society-wide or worldwide issues. Peace in the Middle East? Spiritual revival in the United States and Western Europe? Eradication of the Ebola virus? *Yeah, right*. We also do this with individual, personal issues much closer to home. That couple will reconcile? That mental illness will subside? That family member will come to know Christ? That infertile couple will conceive? You know, in your head, that God is powerful enough to do something about these things. But you also know, in your heart and from your own experience, that God usually doesn't. And so you greet Scripture's impossible promises with a laugh and shrug of the shoulders. *Yeah, right*.

I've even been on the receiving end of this attitude in a way. I remember being in college, at a tennis tournament, and seeing another player whom I had known relatively well in high school. I hadn't seen him in four or five years; and he didn't know that I had experienced a spiritual conversion in my life, much less anything else about the calling I was discerning. As we were catching up, talking about the typical things collegians discuss, he asked what I was planning to do after graduation. My answer was, "I'm going to seminary. I think I'm going to be a minister." I wish you could have seen the deadpan look on this guy's face when I told him that. It had *yeah, right* written all over it. Even the great God couldn't do that with you, Talbot Davis. Maybe God could do it, but I know you and I don't think it will happen. *Yeah, right*.

We've all been there, all felt that in our connection with God. We believe God is great; we just don't believe that God is good. We believe God exists; we just doubt that God will show up.

Which brings us to one of the most fascinating, most significant, and most *yeah right* stories in the whole Bible, when God makes a pretty big promise to Abraham and Sarah in Genesis 18. Abraham and Sarah—the first family of the faith—would have lived sometime between 1500 and 2000 B.C., almost four thousand years ago. This story is old; and at this stage of the story, so are Abraham and Sarah. Abraham is ninety-nine years old, and Sarah is eighty-nine. At God's command, Abraham and Sarah had left their home years before to go to Canaan, the Promised Land that would eventually belong to their descendants, the Israelites. As Genesis 18 opens, Abraham and Sarah are dwelling as foreigners among the inhabitants of the land, living at a place called the oaks of Mamre. They are facing a dilemma, really the major complication of the whole story of Abraham: God has promised to make Abraham the ancestor of a great nation, but he has no children with his wife Sarah (see Genesis 12:1-3; 13:14-18; 15:1-6). Now he does have a son, Ishmael, with Sarah's maidservant Hagar; but that makes for some bad family dynamics (Genesis 16:1-16). God has been clear that Sarah will be the mother of Abraham's chosen lineage (Genesis 17:15-22), even though she has been barren her whole life. Abraham and Sarah find themselves bumping up against this promise from God. So far, they have been over-promised and under-delivered. All that sets the stage for God's appearance to Abraham in Genesis 18:1-15:

> [1] The LORD appeared to Abraham at the oaks of Mamre
> while he sat at the entrance of his tent in the day's heat. [2] He
> looked up and suddenly saw three men standing near him.
> As soon as he saw them, he ran from his tent entrance to
> greet them and bowed deeply. [3] He said, "Sirs, if you would
> be so kind, don't just pass by your servant. [4] Let a little water
> be brought so you may wash your feet and refresh yourselves
> under the tree. [5] Let me offer you a little bread so you will
> feel stronger, and after that you may leave your servant and
> go on your way—since you have visited your servant."

They responded, "Fine. Do just as you have said."

6 So Abraham hurried to Sarah at his tent and said, "Hurry! Knead three seahs of the finest flour and make some baked goods!" 7 Abraham ran to the cattle, took a healthy young calf, and gave it to a young servant, who prepared it quickly. 8 Then Abraham took butter, milk, and the calf that had been prepared, put the food in front of them, and stood under the tree near them as they ate.

9 They said to him, "Where's your wife Sarah?"

And he said, "Right here in the tent."

10 Then one of the men said, "I will definitely return to you about this time next year. Then your wife Sarah will have a son!"

Sarah was listening at the tent door behind him. 11 Now Abraham and Sarah were both very old. Sarah was no longer menstruating. 12 So Sarah laughed to herself, thinking, *I'm no longer able to have children and my husband's old.*

13 The LORD said to Abraham, "Why did Sarah laugh and say, 'Me give birth? At my age?' 14 Is anything too difficult for the LORD? When I return to you about this time next year, Sarah will have a son."

15 Sarah lied and said, "I didn't laugh," because she was frightened.

But he said, "No, you laughed."

The first two verses are confusing when we first read them. Who exactly appears to Abraham? Is it one Lord (verse 1), or three men (verse 2)? The short answer is, yes. It is both. We don't know exactly what is going on here or how it's unfolding, but it seems that Abraham meets an embodied, enfleshed manifestation of God. It's similar to the God in human form who wrestles with Jacob in Genesis 32:22-32. Some of the early church fathers wondered whether this appearance—and others like it in the Old Testament—was some kind of a "pre-Jesus," a preview of the Incarnation, when

God became a human in the person of Jesus of Nazareth. It's also unclear how exactly these three men manifest the one LORD. Is it one God in a single body with two messengers in attendance, or is it an early image of the Trinity: Father, Son, and Holy Spirit? We do not know exactly how it works, but we do know that Abraham receives a visit from God in the form of these three men. And we know that this is both odd and unprecedented.

We also know that in response, Abraham goes into full-speed hospitality mode. Read verses 2-8 closely and notice all of the words having to do with haste: *ran, hurried, hurry, quickly*. All of this urgency shows the visitors how important they are to Abraham. By rushing to serve them, he demonstrates that they have honored him by coming to his tent. Hospitality was important in Abraham's culture, and he wanted to go the extra mile to welcome his guests appropriately.

This level of hospitality is still valued in certain cultures around the world today. I have visited India a few times over the past several years, and it's remarkable how similar this description of Abraham's hospitality is to the experience of a guest in India. It is exceedingly important in that culture to show guests that they are welcomed and honored. It's that kind of treatment that Abraham provides for God here in Genesis 18. He even stands nearby while his guests eat (verse 8), hovering within reach, in case they need anything. Again, it's the same in India: The guests eat while the host hovers. It's the host's way of saying that honoring and welcoming the guests are of utmost importance. Interestingly enough, it doesn't say for sure that Abraham knew that he was welcoming divine visitors; for all he knew, he may well have thought that they were three men weary from the road.

All that changes at verse 9, however, when the guests shift the tone of the meeting dramatically with their question, "Where's your wife Sarah?" Now if the visitors are divine, they already know the answer. If they aren't divine, it's a nervy, inappropriate question to ask. Either way, their question changes the nature of their meeting with Abraham. It doesn't look as though they've come for a simple visit after all.

The answer to their question, "Where's your wife Sarah?" is that Sarah is in her tent, eavesdropping (verse 10). If we were to make a show called *The Real Housewives of Genesis,* eavesdropping would be one of the main devices to advance the plot. Sarah does it here, and Rebekah will do it later (Genesis 27:5), both at key moments in the story. It says in verse 10 that Sarah is listening to Abraham's conversation with the men, from the door of the tent. What Sarah hears as she listens from the tent is news that concerns her: "Then one of the men said, 'I will definitely return to you about this time next year. Then your wife Sarah will have a son!'" (Genesis 18:10).

Isn't that turn of events sort of sad? This is news that Sarah has been waiting all her life to hear—she's going to be a *mother*—and even now she doesn't hear it directly. She only overhears it spoken to someone else, her husband. That's how it was in Sarah's day. She lived in a man's world, where women usually weren't trusted to receive important news even if it concerned them. It was delivered to the men. So Sarah had to eavesdrop to overhear the most important news of her life.

Even as Sarah overhears this promise, the narrator confronts us immediately with the unlikelihood of delivery, telling us in verse 11 that Sarah and Abraham were both old and Sarah had passed the age of childbearing. Now, my mother was forty-six when I was born; and that's pretty old to be having a child. (Of course, she still plays tennis at ninety-nine; so age has never slowed her down.) But forty-six is nothing compared with Sarah's age. If what God says is true, Sarah will be ninety by the time she has her first child. What God promises here is simply not possible from a biological perspective.

So Sarah's response in 18:12 is understandable: "So Sarah laughed to herself, thinking, I'm no longer able to have children and my husband's old." Sarah recognizes that she is old, and the time for bearing children has passed her by. And she can do nothing with God's words and their extraordinary promise, except laugh to herself. I've tried to picture that laugh, to imagine what it would have looked like in the tent when she heard this news and laughed to herself. I think it it's something like *Humph . . . yeah, right*. When I picture it, I imagine a sarcastic little grin. It's the same laugh I use when chronic no-show parishioners tell me, "See ya Sunday;" it's the same one you use when a politician makes fanciful promises. *Yeah, right*. Sarah feels that same natural cynicism we do when confronted with the tried-and-true certainty that what is promised will not materialize.

You could, God, but you won't. The odds of this actually happening are just too long. You might have created nature and reproduction, but I haven't seen you bend the rules of nature once in all my eighty-nine years. I'm too old; and that promise just gets a laugh, a great big "yeah, right."

SARAH'S LAUGHING DOUBT IS OUR DOUBT AS WELL.

I know that's exactly where many of us are today with the deepest needs and the greatest obstacles that we face. We hear the slightest bit of hope, the slightest promise that God is going to show up and make things better, and we react as Sarah did: *yeah, right*. We tell ourselves that the marriage will just keep spiraling out of control. Or we laugh to ourselves that our "single" status will never change because we're not the right person or we haven't found the right person. You and I laugh hope away because the situation is too immense and the promise feels too impossible. For me, on occasion, it involves the church I serve. I think about all of the untapped potential of Good Shepherd Church, even with all that God has already accomplished in us and through us, and the possibility that we would live up to that potential. I think about the possibility that I can be the kind of leader to make that happen. Sometimes when I think about all of that, I respond *yeah, right*.

We've all done it. We shrug our shoulders at God's promises in our lives because the alternative is too impossible to consider seriously. Sarah's laughing doubt to herself is our doubt as well.

But the story goes on, as we see in 18:13: "The LORD said to Abraham, 'Why did Sarah laugh . . . ?'" Woops, caught in the act! The irony here is that Abraham had done the exact same thing in the chapter before. He also had gotten news that Sarah would bear a son, and he also laughed when he heard it, but he suffered no reprimand from God (17:17). Sarah receives no such grace; God calls her out for her inner thoughts of doubt and dismissal. To make matters worse, she *lies* about it. In verse 15, she says, "I didn't laugh," because she is afraid. And the narrator doesn't sugarcoat it, telling us bluntly that "Sarah lied." She tries to cover it up—nope, that's not my hand in the cookie jar! No wonder the church is so messed up, when these are our ancestors of faith—Abraham and Sarah, liars and schemers even when they're talking to God. Of course, God sees right through Sarah's lie, directly confronting her with the truth: "No, you laughed" (verse 15).

WHEN YOU SNEER, "YEAH, RIGHT," GOD SAYS, "WATCH THIS!"

However, in between Sarah's laughing (verse 12) and her lying (verse 15), between the crime and the cover-up is this little gem that makes all of the difference. God says in verse 14, "Is anything too difficult for the LORD?" Is *anything* too supernatural for God to accomplish? Is anything too unbelievable or too great for God to do? Is it too hard for the Lord to bend the laws of nature? Of course not. The One who wrote the laws of nature can surely edit them. God reminds Abraham, and Sarah who is listening in, that nothing lies beyond the Lord's power. As if to emphasize this truth, God repeats the promise that caused Sarah to laugh in the first place: "When I return to you about this time next year, Sarah will have a son" (verse 14). Sarah is going to have that boy. Her laughter and even her lying does not end her conversation with God. She might not believe it, but God is not finished with her yet. God can overcome her cynicism, her laughing, because God is doing something bigger than she is. Is anything too hard for the Lord?

In spite of Sarah's laughing disbelief, God reiterates the promise to Abraham and Sarah with the challenge, "Is anything too difficult for the LORD?" And the whole story—Abraham's hopping hospitality, God's outlandish prediction, Sarah's laugh and her lie—lands us here: ***When you sneer, "Yeah, right," God says, "Watch this!"***

When your sarcasm and cynicism rule the day and say it can't happen, God says, "Watch this!" God is not only great; God is also good: *Watch this*. God's desire and interest do match God's ability: *Watch this*. God's nature is loving kindness, making a way where there seems to be no way: *Watch this*.

The claim of Genesis 18:14, "Is anything too difficult for the LORD," is a character trait of God for us to hold on to. It is a part of God's nature that we are called and invited to embrace. It's not just a promise to believe; it's a trait for us to cling to. There is a big difference between the two. If you believe that God is great but doubt that God is good, I am not suggesting you start claiming nature-bending miracles as your birthright before they even happen. What I am suggesting is that you embrace God's character trait—"Is anything too difficult for the LORD"—trusting in God's greatness, faithfulness, goodness, and wisdom. Even when the laws of nature don't bend your way, you hold on to the knowledge that nothing is beyond God's power and love; that steadfast trust is how you endure. What God tells Sarah and Abraham, and what God tells us, is that God can be trusted even when life is falling apart. It's more than a promise we believe; it's an aspect of the divine nature in which we place our faith.

I have to confess something: I cry every time I sing the song *Our God*. Whether we sing it at Good Shepherd Church or somewhere else, the song always moves me deeply. It's because of some parents at our church whom I love dearly. A while back these parents lost a child; and at the funeral for their child, they insisted that we sing *Our God,* which praises God as "greater . . . stronger . . . higher than any other." I cannot sing that song without seeing that mother and father at the funeral for their child, with their hands up in the air, singing to the Lord. I cannot hear the song without thinking of their integrity, their endurance, and their deep trust in God's goodness through it all. Their child died; the laws of nature weren't reversed for them. But the beauty of the Spirit continues to come through for them.

GOD HAS THE LAST LAUGH.

Can you be trusted with that powerful character trait of God? Can you be trusted to move away from cynicism and sarcastic dismissal of God's promises? I hope that you will hold on to that aspect of God's nature that says, "Is anything too difficult for the Lord?" I hope that you will recognize that just because humans over-promise and under-deliver, it doesn't mean that God does too.

Trying circumstances like what Sarah faced can cause us to doubt, dismissing God's promises with a scornful laugh. But we can respond to that type of doubt by leaning on God's very nature, staying on the lookout for God's grace in whatever form it might come. God's Genesis 18:14 miracle may be to sustain you and bless you through circumstances that do not change. I hope that you won't be the type of person who laughs, *yeah, right,* believing that God's grace might exist for others but not for you. I hope that you will be like the person of faith responding to a skeptic who asked why she believed in God. Her answer was, "Because I'm alive." She knew that her very life was testimony to God's power and ability to come through for her. Sometimes that knowledge is enough. We will never see the whole picture, never understand why sometimes God answers miraculously and sometimes does not. But we do know God's character, that nothing is too hard for the Lord.

All of this brings us back to Sarah and her *yeah right*. The story continues, and we must read on in Genesis to find out the outcome of God's promise and Sarah's laughing doubt. Genesis 18 isn't complete without Genesis 21:1-6:

> 1 The LORD was attentive to Sarah just as he had said, and
> the LORD carried out just what he had promised her. 2 She
> became pregnant and gave birth to a son for Abraham when
> he was old, at the very time God had told him. 3 Abraham
> named his son—the one Sarah bore him—Isaac. 4 Abraham
> circumcised his son Isaac when he was eight days old just
> as God had commanded him. 5 Abraham was 100 years old
> when his son Isaac was born. 6 Sarah said, "God has given me
> laughter. Everyone who hears about it will laugh with me."

"God has given me laughter. Everyone who hears about it will laugh with me" (Genesis 21:6). God fulfills the promise, making Sarah pregnant and giving her a son: "just what he had promised her" (Genesis 21:1). The boy's name is Isaac, which means "He laughs" or simply "Laughter." *Laughter. One who laughs. Laugh with me*. God transforms Sarah's laughter. No longer is the derisive *yeah, right* laugh of disbelief on her lips. Now Sarah laughs with joy, her heart full of delight at God's fulfillment of the impossible promise. Her sneer turns into a celebration. For the rest of Sarah's life, Isaac will be a continual reminder for her not to underestimate God. Whenever Sarah sees the little boy Laughter running around, she will remember how God said, "Watch this," in response to her *yeah, right*. Simply by virtue of his presence in her life, Isaac will be a perpetual sign to Sarah: don't sell God short.

You, too, have continual reminders in your life not to underestimate God. Open your eyes to see them whenever you start to sneer *yeah, right*. That marriage that is still intact despite huge obstacles. That addiction that is in remission and recovery. That faith you have today, God's presence in your life when there's no earthly reason to explain it. I have the people of Good Shepherd United Methodist Church. Together we have the cross, the ultimate symbol of defeat and death that God has turned into a symbol of victory and life. All of us who know Christ have these reminders and others—large and small, global and personal—to urge us not to underestimate God. Through them, we can celebrate that nothing is too difficult for the Lord. We, like Sarah, can remember time and again that God has the last laugh.

Questions for Reflection and Discussion

Write responses and other thoughts in the space below each question. If you are discussing the book in a small group, prepare for the meeting by writing answers in advance.

1. In what areas of your life have you experienced "over-promise and under-deliver?" Responses may range from mundane issues, such as restaurants or technology, to big-picture matters such as politics or the church.

2. In what ways have you noticed that you can over-promise and under-deliver?

3. What does Abraham's concern for hospitality for his guests say about his character? Did he know that his visitors were divine right away? How would this make a difference in how you interpret his hospitality?

4. Reread the scene in which Sarah laughs at God's promise that she would have a son. What thoughts or emotions do you think gave rise to her laughter? When have you had similar feelings or thoughts?

5. Why, do you think, did Sarah lie when confronted about her laughter? How else might she have responded?

6. The Bible depicts a change in Sarah's disposition, from cynicism in Genesis 18 to joy and delight in Genesis 21. Did this change come about suddenly or gradually? How do you think her joy at Isaac's birth affected her outlook on life going forward?

7. Think about all of the promises and reasons for hope that we find in Scripture. Which of these are most likely to cause you to say, "Yeah, right"?

8. What situation exists in your life where it is difficult to imagine God making things better anytime soon? In what way are you waiting for God to say, "Watch this"? What hope can you draw from Sarah's story?

9. Have you ever experienced God bending the laws of nature? If so, how and where did this happen? What was your response?

10. Recall a time when God completely took you by surprise by intervening in your life. How can you draw strength from that in light of obstacles you're presently facing?

11. How is God seeking to move you from cynicism to joy? How can you surrender to this process and cooperate with God in doing so?

What Does Grace Look Like?

Draw a picture of grace. On a blank sheet of paper, use a pencil, markers, crayons, or whatever is available to draw a picture of what God's grace looks like in your life. Focus on a personal, specific instance or instances of grace that you have witnessed or experienced. Alternatively, search on a smart phone for a photograph or work of art that captures the meaning of grace for you. If you are part of a group study, have each group member share his or her picture and explain why it's a portrait of grace. As you look at the pictures, meditate for a few minutes on the question, "Is anything too difficult for the Lord?" Hold on to these pictures as a reminder of God's greatness and goodness.

Closing Prayer

Eternal God, nothing is too difficult for you. We've been disappointed by people and circumstances, and the Scriptures are full of promises that seem too wonderful and impossible for us to trust. But we know that with you, nothing is impossible. We cling to those things that remind us of your strength and goodness. Give us courage to hope in you even in when we are tempted to dismiss your promises. When humans or situations let us down, help us put our faith in you and see your deep, life-changing grace. Amen.

Daily Scripture Readings

This week, read the following Scripture passages. Immerse yourself in Sarah's and Abraham's story, considering all that God did for them and how they responded to it.

Monday: Genesis 12:1-20
Tuesday: Genesis 15:1–16:16
Wednesday: Genesis 17:1-27
Thursday: Genesis 18:1-33
Friday: Genesis 21:1-21

4

LIFE AFTER LOSS

"The Lord has given; the Lord has taken; bless the Lord's name." (Job 1:21)

The Book of Job is about loss. It's about suffering and the questions, anger, and doubts that go along with it. That makes it ideal to help us understand life after loss, how we can go on living in faith after suffering a loss that defies measurement.

I have to tell you something that most people have gotten completely wrong about the Bible. It involves a phrase that almost everyone knows and uses; it's a phrase that, I must confess, I know and have used myself. Ready? Here it is: *the patience of Job*. Whenever we see someone endure difficult people or situations with a great attitude, we declare that he or she has "the patience of Job." This common phrase is based on the story of Job, which we find in the biblical book of the same name. Those who use the phrase uphold Job as a model of patience, the ultimate figure of faithfulness and endurance in the face of hardship.

Except, that's just not right. It's based on a terribly wrong reading of that particular story. The Job we meet in the Bible was many things—wealthy, devout, angry, frustrated, long-winded, grieving, nervy, long-winded again—but patient is not one of them. To be sure, Job is patient at first . . . for about two chapters out of a book that's forty-two chapters long. But when we get to chapter three, Job curses the day he was born (Job 3:1). Over and over he complains bitterly, protesting that he is innocent and his suffering is undeserved. Eventually, he goes so far as to demand that God show up and deliver a written indictment for Job's sins that warrant his suffering (Job 31:35). To lift up "the patience of Job" as an ideal is to stop at Job 2. That phrase is a great misunderstanding of the man and his book, and we do a disservice to both when we propagate it.

Job is actually much more interesting and complex than the usual identification as a "patient" man describes him. It starts with his very name. "Job" is not an Israelite name; in fact, it's hard to identify it by any nationality of the time. The character Job was known as a traditional figure across many ancient cultures; already when the Book of Job was written, the name would have had a foreign, almost archaic ring to it. This is the Bible's way of saying, among other things, that what's about to happen to him could happen to *anyone*. Job's story is not a Hebrew story or a Jewish story or Christian story; it's a human story. It's our story.

JOB'S STORY IS OUR STORY.

It's hard to isolate a single short passage from Job, because it really takes the whole book to tell the complete story. Job undergoes some severe hardship in chapters 1 and 2, and he argues about it with some of his friends in chapters 3 through 37. God appears and speaks to Job in chapters 38–41, then Job answers God in chapter 42. Finally, God restores Job's fortunes at the end of the book, the second half of chapter 42. It's a long book, with a lot of twists and turns and arguments, with an ending that's not exactly satisfying. But we can look at Job 1 to get a general overview of the book. It provides a starting point to discuss Job's suffering and his response, and how Job's story can help us address the doubt that comes from loss. Here is Job 1, which opens with an introduction of Job and his great piety and wealth:

> 1 A man in the land of Uz was named Job. That man
> was honest, a person of absolute integrity; he feared God
> and avoided evil. 2 He had seven sons and three daughters,
> 3 and owned seven thousand sheep, three thousand camels,
> five hundred pairs of oxen, five hundred female donkeys,
> and a vast number of servants, so that he was greater than
> all the people of the east. 4 Each of his sons hosted a feast
> in his own house on his birthday. They invited their three
> sisters to eat and drink with them. 5 When the days of the
> feast had been completed, Job would send word and purify
> his children. Getting up early in the morning, he prepared
> entirely burned offerings for each one of them, for Job
> thought, Perhaps my children have sinned and then cursed
> God in their hearts. Job did this regularly.
>
> 6 One day the divine beings came to present themselves
> before the LORD, and the Adversary also came among them.
> 7 The LORD said to the Adversary, "Where did you come from?"
>
> The Adversary answered the LORD, "From wandering
> throughout the earth."
>
> 8 The LORD said to the Adversary, "Have you thought
> about my servant Job; surely there is no one like him on
> earth, a man who is honest, who is of absolute integrity,
> who reveres God and avoids evil?"
>
> 9 The Adversary answered the LORD, "Does Job revere
> God for nothing? 10 Haven't you fenced him in—his house
> and all he has—and blessed the work of his hands so that
> his possessions extend throughout the earth? 11 But stretch

> out your hand and strike all he has. He will certainly curse you to your face."
>
> 12 The LORD said to the Adversary, "Look, all he has is within your power; only don't stretch out your hand against him." So the Adversary left the LORD's presence.
>
> 13 One day Job's sons and daughters were eating and drinking wine in their oldest brother's house. 14 A messenger came to Job and said: "The oxen were plowing, and the donkeys were grazing nearby 15 when the Sabeans took them and killed the young men with swords. I alone escaped to tell you."
>
> 16 While this messenger was speaking, another arrived and said: "A raging fire fell from the sky and burned up the sheep and devoured the young men. I alone escaped to tell you."
>
> 17 While this messenger was speaking, another arrived and said: "Chaldeans set up three companies, raided the camels and took them, killing the young men with swords. I alone escaped to tell you."
>
> 18 While this messenger was speaking, another arrived and said: "Your sons and your daughters were eating and drinking wine in their oldest brother's house, 19 when a strong wind came from the desert and struck the four corners of the house. It fell upon the young people, and they died. I alone escaped to tell you."
>
> 20 Job arose, tore his clothes, shaved his head, fell to the ground, and worshipped. 21 He said: "Naked I came from my mother's womb; naked I will return there. The LORD has given; the LORD has taken; bless the LORD's name."
>
> 22 In all this, Job didn't sin or blame God.

After introducing the reader to Job and his great wealth (Job 1:1-5), the Book of Job opens on a scene in the divine throne room. God's attendants are presenting themselves before the Lord, and one such being, called the Adversary, enters into a dialogue with God (Job 1:6-12). Some translations call this being Satan or The Satan, but it is important to recognize this is not the devil, the supreme evil power of Christian thought. Although the Hebrew literally says, "The Satan," this is simply the name of a member of God's divine council, whose role it was to bring accusations against those who have sinned against God. So "The Adversary" or "The Accuser" is the best way to translate this Hebrew word. As an analogy, one might think of this being like the prosecutor in a courtroom. God invites this being, the Adversary, to consider Job; it's almost as if God is bragging about Job's uprightness and goodness.

The Adversary replies that Job fears God because he has received nothing but good things. Job has every reason to worship God faithfully, the Adversary points out, because God has blessed Job beyond measure. The Adversary tells God that Job's attitude will change very quickly if his wealth and prosperity are taken away (Job 1:11). As a result of this conversation, God and the Adversary reach a deal that the *reader* of the story knows about, but Job does not (Job 1:12). There's dramatic irony in which audience knows what is going on, but the character Job is ignorant. And in this deal, God gives the Adversary free reign to test Job with hardship.

OF ALL THE SHADOWS OF DOUBT WE FACE, DOUBTS BORN OF LOSS ARE THE MOST ACUTE.

To say that the test is severe would be an understatement. In short order, Job loses his servants, his livestock, and then, most cruelly, his sons and daughters (Job 1:13-19). Job loses one thing after another in rapid succession, some to bandits and others to natural disasters. The news about one catastrophe is still coming in when the report of the next arrives. It all happens in a single day; seven biblical verses reduce Job, father of ten and wealthiest man alive, to a childless man with no property to speak of.

Job experiences a loss—or rather, a series of losses—that defy measurement. He loses all of those belongings and, much more critically, all those people in such a short span of time. How can we possibly quantify what Job experiences? The Bible goes to great lengths to overstate Job's enormous wealth, as though to emphasize just how staggering it is when everything is suddenly gone. People talk so often about "the patience of Job," but that's not what the book or the man is about at all. Job is a lot less about "patience" than it is about "loss." Losses you cannot measure.

Of all the shadows of doubt we face, doubts born of loss are the most acute. They are some of the doubts I see most often in ministry, in the community, in the church and outside of the church. In chapter one I mentioned the Facebook poll where I asked people about the sources of their doubts. It's no coincidence that matters of loss and suffering were among the most frequently mentioned sources of doubt. Whether our losses are communal or personal, they can shake our faith to the core. Loss that defies measure can cause deep doubts among even the most faithful of people. When we have something so valuable—property, status, a relationship, a loved one—and it is suddenly gone, how do we survive? How do we persevere? How do we keep our faith? How do we emerge from the shadow of doubt when the things or the people we love the most are suddenly taken from us?

There are all kinds of loss, ranging from the trivial to the catastrophic. As a preacher, I hate to lose an audience. To be speaking and *know* that you're not connecting, to think to yourself "I'm dying up here"—that's a tough loss. I guess that's why a university professor I heard of would come to lecture every day and pull a tennis ball out of his jacket. He never said a word about the tennis ball; he'd just place that it on the podium as he lectured. And no one ever knew why. Until one day, one of his students fell asleep in class. The professor didn't miss a word of his lecture while he walked back to the podium, picked up the tennis ball, and *whomp*! He threw it and nailed the poor guy right on his sleepy head. It shocked the whole class, especially the sleeping student. The next day, the professor walked into the room, reached into his jacket, and pulled out a baseball. No one ever fell asleep in his class again. That's loss prevention!

But of course, there's more than losing an audience. Some people have lost hair. That's tough, I know, especially when it is due to cancer or another serious disease. Other people have lost jobs, and have lost more than income and benefits along with them. "How can I go on," many wonder, "without the sense of self that is wrapped up in my job?" People lose valuables, misplacing a wedding ring or some other treasure with a lot of personal meaning attached to it. I have been there a couple of times watching a house burn while standing next to the church members who own it. How do you recover from the loss of so many things and so many precious memories?

Others have lost a marriage—a marriage that they thought they'd have literally until death parted them. And then, how well do I know that there are those who've lost parents, spouses, and children. In the wake of all of these losses and the myriad others that people experience, how in the world can we go on having faith? How do we have faith in life after loss? Job's story is our story—loss that defies measure.

Since his story is our story, we could learn from Job. Look at how he responds to the pile-on of bad news in verses 20-21: "Job arose, tore his clothes, shaved his head, fell to the ground, and worshipped. He said: 'Naked I came from my mother's womb; naked I will return there. The LORD has given; the LORD has taken; bless the LORD's name.'" As marvelous as Job's words are—and we'll get to them in a bit—his *actions* speak louder to me. Job tore his clothes and shaved his head, which seems odd to our minds. What is that all about? As strange as these actions might seem to us, they were in fact ancient Hebrew customs of showing grief. They were a way to give physical, tangible expression to the rage one felt at the world and to the frustration one felt with God. Job's behavior was a vivid, dramatic way to tell God, "I've had enough of this!"

Readers of Job are often tempted to skip straight to Job's words in verse 21, without recognizing his actions in verse 20. Job did not

GOD PREFERS YOUR ANGER OVER YOUR ISOLATION.

deny that bad things had happened to him. He did not put on a happy face or keep a stiff upper lip. Job did not bear it all with cheerful patience or remind himself that it was likely all for the best. By his actions, Job gave *expression* to the anger he felt but couldn't articulate.

It's important also for us to read verse 22, which declares that Job did not sin "in all this," through his actions or his words. Job expressed to God and to others his grief and his anger, and it was not sinful for him to do so. Do you know what I get from that vivid, impatient demonstration—for those of us wrestling with life after loss? ***God prefers your anger over your isolation.***

Sometimes when we face life's unfairness, the reality of our losses, and the doubts that arise as a result, the healthiest thing we can do is vent. We can tear our clothes and be honest with God about our anger. Job's anger escalates throughout the rest of the book; he eventually challenges God about the legitimacy of his suffering, denying that his losses are deserved. Remarkably, God appears and speaks to Job, essentially reprimanding him for speaking about things he has no knowledge or authority to question. In the end, though, God vindicates Job and restores his fortunes (Job 42:7-17). Although Job speaks out of turn by questioning God, it does not end Job's relationship with the Lord. It's similar to what we saw in the psalms in Chapter 1: We can be honest about where we are, even when that involves severe doubts and anger. *God prefers your anger over your isolation.*

Why would I say such a thing? After all, being angry with God is a radical thing to read about in a Christian book, much more so coming from the pen of a preacher. But as we saw in chapter one, anger at God does show up in the Bible—the psalms are full of angry words directed at God. The chosen people, the Israelites, are those whose namesake wrestled with God. Job expressed his anger with God, first with torn clothes and a shaved head and later with angry words. In each of these instances, the anger humans felt toward God did not have the last word. Anger or struggle did not end the relationship between the people and the Lord. God does not turn away from the Israelites, or the psalmists, or Job because of their anger. And we can rest assured that when we give a voice to our anger, God will not turn away from us either. God can take our anger and frustration. God is not intimidated or offended by it.

On the other hand, when we ignore God and turn our backs on faith, it breaks God's heart. And that's exactly what many folks do in the wake of a major loss. They decide that God doesn't exist. Or they live as though they have decided that God doesn't exist. Profound loss leads to profound hurt, anger, and frustration. Many respond by isolating themselves from God: ceasing to worship or worshipping less regularly; praying less; giving or serving less; praising God less often or with less joy. I've seen it happen to people I know. You may have seen it, too; or maybe you have lived it. Losses that defy measure can lead us to turn our backs on God. I wonder whether the hollowness of that response comes, in part, because we don't feel the freedom and intimacy with God to tear our clothes, admit our anger, and really let God know how we feel. Isolation from God keeps us in the shadows of doubt, but expressing our anger toward God is one way for us to bring our doubts out of the shadows and into the light. God can handle it. *God prefers your anger over your isolation.*

Here's the theological truth behind that: When we vent our anger with God, we acknowledge that God is in charge. God is sovereign. Look at Job's words in the second half of Job 1:21, after he has expressed his anger physically: "Naked I came from my mother's womb; naked I will return there. The LORD has given; the LORD has taken; bless the LORD's name." Such words and such a concept are really hard to wrap our minds around. Job acknowledges that God is in control even in the face of pain and loss. God is not powerless and helpless before evil and chaos. God is sovereign over life's troubles as well as life's joys. God gives. *And God takes.*

We see this notion of God's sovereignty in Job's words in 1:21; and if we read on in Job, we find it through the rest of the book as well. In other ancient religions that existed when the Book of Job was written, the forces of chaos such as storms, death, beasts, and the deep were portrayed as *enemies* of the gods. Almost as though two great, equal cosmic forces were at work in our world: God or the gods, on the one hand, and the personified forces of chaos on the other. This was a common view of the world, and some version of it was shared by many of the peoples who surrounded the ancient Hebrews. Well, it was not so with the Bible in general or with Job in particular. In the Bible, there are no such cosmic enemies of God, nothing in creation that can rival God's power. Job mentions two mighty, terrifying creatures, Leviathan and Behemoth, which sound as if they are chaos monsters. They have some parallels with the personified forces of chaos we see in other ancient religions. But in Job, the Lord created even these beings, and they are subject to God (Job 40:15–41:34). All pieces of creation are under God's authority; even the chaotic forces act only by God's permission.

This is a completely different way of understanding God's absolute power than what we see in the other ancient religions; it is part of the Bible's witness that there is only one God. Some Christian denominations recognize this more readily than others. Methodists aren't as comfortable with notion of God's supreme authority as are our Presbyterian friends, but the Presbyterians have something to show us. As they well know, God is sovereign and in control. Even of chaos. Even of loss. God gives and God takes. We want to excuse God from that since it's easier to minimize God than it is to enlarge our hearts. But Job and his words move us to a different place. In the wake of deep loss, Job's words ask us: Can you radically trust the same God *who could have prevented it*? Can you? God could have prevented that divorce, that death, that illness, that job loss. Can you trust God even though it happened anyway?

JOB NEVER LEARNS THE REASON FOR HIS SUFFERING.

So why did it happen? Why didn't God prevent your loss, whatever that might have been, that stays with you, brings you anger, and moves you to doubt? That is the question that lies at the heart of the Book of Job: Why does Job suffer even though he is a righteous man who fears God and does no wrong? Job doesn't ask it in chapter one, but he and his friends discuss it at length through the rest of the book. They go round and round the question for more than thirty chapters. Job's friends say that Job must have done something wrong, that his suffering must be deserved, while Job maintains his innocence and righteousness. Remember: The reader knows about the deal God has made with the Adversary in Job 1, but Job and his friends do not. And what we long for as we read is for God to show up and tell poor Job about the test. If only he could hear from God that it was a test, surely it would put his mind at ease.

Except that never happens. God does show up at the end of the book (Job 38–41), but God never lets Job in on the secret. Instead, God chastises Job for speaking about things he cannot possibly understand. God has created the world and everything in it, but where was Job when God laid the foundations of the earth (Job 38:4)? Job questions God over and over, his anger turning into a demand for an answer to his most basic question: "Why?" And as the reader knows, there is a reason. We can debate whether it's a good reason, but there is a reason; and odds are that knowing it will satisfy Job's need for an answer. But God never tells Job; Job never learns the reason for his suffering. Job must respond without knowing all of the facts, without ever understanding why.

Isn't that so very much like our experience with loss? We never know why profound losses happen, not really. If Job had received a good answer from God, his story would no longer be our story. Instead, he stays in the dark, as we do most of the time.

There may be reasons for our losses, and maybe we can guess them. Perhaps God allows disappointment in our lives as a way of diminishing the glamor and bright lights of the world, to expand our trust in God. Or perhaps loss reminds us that we've got idols to deal with, and anything we make into an idol can be taken away. There is even value in the pain that we go through in loss. You may have heard of a disease called congenital analgesia, which is a rare condition that leaves people with no sensitivity for pain. Because they don't feel pain, they injure themselves with extraordinary frequency: Children can bite off the tips of their fingers, burn their hands severely, and even break bones. Pain now prevents greater trouble later. Something like that could be why loss exists. With me, I know that God has given me frustration in ministry or a sense of plateau in order to drive me to my knees in prayer. I don't think that I've lost anything more serious than momentum in ministry, but it got me to recover my first love. God keeps turning me into the widow from Luke 18 who would not stop badgering the judge until she got what she wanted. God wants me that persistent in prayer.

But all these reasons we can come up with—and there are many, many more—will never completely explain our losses. Like Job, we will never know why they happen. Job and his friends may have raised all sorts of possible reasons for Job's suffering, but a divine deal with the Adversary to test Job wasn't on anybody's radar. Job can't possibly understand the workings of the world to know the mind of God, the reason why everything happens. And get this: God doesn't tell him, because *God doesn't answer to Job*. And God doesn't answer to us either. Like Job, we must respond to loss, without ever knowing the full reason. Will we isolate ourselves from God, allowing anger to give way to doubt? Or will we express our anger, bringing our doubts and our frustrations out of the shadows and into the light?

By they way, many people are not in the middle of a major loss at the moment. Others may not even be able to look back upon such an experience in their past. A few may even make it through life in such a way that Job's story is only ever hypothetical; they will never know the kind of traumatic loss that gives rise to so much doubt and anger. But no matter who you are and what your own experience has been or will be, virtually all of us will know someone going through a loss that can't be measured. Death, divorce, depression, and other forms of suffering are so common that we'll all know someone who has experienced that type of loss. When that happens and we wonder how to respond and what to say, we should remember Job's three friends.

Three of Job's friends rush to his side when they hear of the calamity that has befallen him at the outset of Job's story. I'm sure that they have Tupperware in tow, like good Methodists. And as far as the end of chapter 2 goes, they're doing well: "They sat with Job on the ground seven days and seven nights, not speaking a word to him, for they saw that he was in excruciating pain" (Job 2:13). But Job doesn't end at the conclusion of chapter 2. There are forty more chapters left to go. And much of those chapters are full of the three friends talking, usually trying to explain to Job why his suffering has come upon him. That's when the three friends transition from being ministers to being windbags. Don't repeat their mistake. When you're trying to help someone who has suffered loss, the ministry of silent presence is the way to go. Don't blow it by trying to explain the inexplicable.

Now, I could end this message with a tidy bow. I could tell you the story of someone who underwent immeasurable loss and then vented their anger at God and came out on the other side with great restoration. That happens sometimes. I pray that it happens to you if you suffer this type of loss. But it's also just a little too easy, a little too facile. Often, life works out that way: it also works the other way just as often.

ANGER GIVES WAY TO WORSHIP.

Instead, look at the last phrase of Job 1:20: After Job tore his clothes and shaved his head, he "fell to the ground, and worshipped." Job's anger at God ultimately gives way to the worship of God. Job chooses to praise the One who could have prevented his loss, because there is no one else in whom Job can believe. Job worships God precisely because God is strong enough and sovereign enough to prevent anything, even though God chooses not to prevent everything. God's ways and decisions may be inscrutable, but using his lungs and hands to worship God is well within Job's ability. And it is within our ability, too, regardless of where we stand or how much we have lost. Job and his friend get nowhere by asking why Job has suffered. But Job worships God anyway, seeking to live faithfully in spite of his suffering.

God prefers our anger over our isolation; and when we have given voice to our anger, it is easier to worship God even though loss remains. Expressing our frustration, bringing our raging doubts into the light, we take a step toward healing ourselves and restoring our own faith and trust in the Lord.

Moving from anger back to worship is a little like that time I went to Abilene, Texas, from my home in Dallas. I was nine years old and my family drove from Dallas to Abilene for a big tennis tournament. Have you ever driven to Abilene? It's not in the middle of nowhere; it *is* nowhere. It took forever. There was nothing but long, flat, featureless landscape that seemed to my nine-year-old brain to be endless. It was a long and hard trip, as I experienced it; I didn't think that we would ever get there.

A few days later, we drove back home from Abilene. And do you know what? It was done in snap. It felt like a short, easy trip; I was surprised at how fast we got back to Dallas after the endless trip to Abilene. Isn't that the way it always works? When we go on a long trip, it always takes a lot less time to come back than it does to get there.

So it is when we come back to worship God in the wake of loss and doubt after we've vented our anger or even turned away from him. Because God is big, vast, and sovereign, able to endure our anger and our doubts that come from it. And God is also intimate, warm, inviting, and always more eager to receive us home than we are to return.

Questions for Reflection and Discussion

Write responses and other thoughts in the space below each question. If you are discussing the book in a small group, prepare for the meeting by writing answers in advance.

1. What are your typical responses when you endure loss in your life? Which types of loss are the hardest for you to experience and confront? What challenges your faith most?

2. When you think of losses that are too great to measure, what sorts of things come to your mind? Why do these things cause doubt so readily?

3. What surprises you most about Job's response to the great loss he suffers? Do you consider Job to be a patient man? Why, or why not?

4. As you consider the message above and the daily Scripture readings below, how do you think Job and the biblical authors arrived at a place of such honesty with God? What would it take for you to be similarly honest and intimate with God?

5. What does it mean for you that God both gives and takes away? How does this notion shape your understanding of God?

6. Recall a time when you navigated loss through the help of God. How did God help you? What was the result?

7. What can you learn about helping others in their time of need through the example of Job's friends in Job 2?

8. Based on this chapter and your own experience, why do loss and suffering happen? How does it affect your faith to hear the answer that the Book of Job seems to give to this question?

9. If "why?" isn't the best question for us to ask God during times of loss, what questions should we ask? How can these other questions help us move past the doubts that loss raises?

Tear It Up

On a piece of paper or fabric, write down a loss you have suffered that has caused you to doubt God or to become angry at God. Or if you have not experienced this type of immeasurable loss, write down a loss that someone you know has suffered. If you are reading this book in a study group, ask everyone to share what they have written so far as they are comfortable doing so. Be aware that not everyone may choose to share.

When you have finished writing and sharing the experience of loss, tear the fabric or paper in two as a way to symbolize your anger and frustration. Note that the tearing is not a form of letting go; it does not make the loss go away. It is rather an expression of anger, a way to show yourself and God how you feel about the loss you have endured.

After you have torn the fabric or paper, pray the prayer below. May you find peace in worshiping the one who gives and takes away.

Closing Prayer

Sovereign God, loss and suffering make us angry and cause us to doubt your goodness and your power. Give us the courage to be honest with you, even angry with you, trusting that it won't stop your love for us. Move us to worship you, seeking to live faithfully in the wake of loss rather than turning our backs on you. Amen.

Daily Scripture Readings

This week, read the following Scripture passages. Pay attention to the perspectives they offer on loss.

Monday: Psalm 22:1-31
Tuesday: 1 Timothy 6:3-10
Wednesday: 2 Corinthians 1:1-5
Thursday: 1 Samuel 2:1-10
Friday: Psalm 6:1-10

5

DOUBT'S BIG BANG

Fools say in their hearts, There is no God. (Psalm 14:1)

We like finding out where things come from, don't we? We like to know the *origins* of things. When we see something that we don't understand, one of the first and most important questions we ask is, "Where did it come from?" That question is the source of some of humankind's most intense scientific speculation: Where did our world come from? Where did the universe in which our world exists come from? Where did our particular human species come from? Scientists have reached some kind of consensus that in the recesses of time there was an event called the *Big Bang,* where everything erupted and expanded from an infinitely small point. Everything in our universe, including the world and our human species, ultimately came from this Big Bang. Agnostics or atheists tend to give the Big Bang a purely scientific explanation, while people of faith say that God was the source of it. In other words, God spoke—BANG—and it was.

This isn't a chapter about Creation; I start with the Big Bang simply to illustrate how deeply interested we all are in origins.

Beginnings. We ask "where did it come from" of all kinds of things, including the universe. We inquire about the beginning of good things and evil things, beautiful things and ugly things. Where did HIV originate? Where does the beauty of the monarch butterfly come from? Where do mosquitoes come from? (Wetlands is where.) What parent with an eight, nine, or ten year old hasn't dreaded the inevitable moment when the child will ask, "Where do babies come from?" This chapter is also not about human reproduction (thankfully). But it does show that we humans are curious about origins even from a very early age. We want to know the source of things, and we'll often do serious investigation—or relentlessly pester mom and dad—until we figure out where things come from.

WHERE DOES DOUBT COME FROM?

So perhaps it's human nature also to wonder where doubts come from. We've been exploring doubt together over the last several chapters, bringing them into the open rather than hiding them in the shadows. In this final chapter, I want to address the origins of doubt, or at least a certain type of doubt. Have you ever been curious about where doubt comes from, particularly doubt about the Christian faith? Face it: We all have doubts about our faith on some level. That's why this way of life is called the Christian *faith,* not the Christian *certainty*. But what is the source of our doubt? Is doubt just the flip side of faith, something that naturally accompanies our trust in something that we can't always see or feel? Partly, yes. We can boldly confront our doubts, bringing them into the light as we have done in this study, because they are a natural companion to belief; we can and should learn to live with a measure of doubt without letting it overcome our faith. There are those doubts and uncertainties that we are content to live with. I've got mine, such as: *What happens to the souls of people who never hear about Christ?* Is that a place where I live in the shadow of doubt? You bet. Will it wreck my faith? No. There are some doubts where we just have to live in tension and trust God for the rest.

But there's another kind of doubt, a more serious kind of doubt, that does threaten to unravel faith. It casts a much larger, much darker shadow over our relationship with Christ. I think that this type of doubt can be traced to a Big Bang of sorts. It's the kind of doubt you may have seen or gone through in college. Maybe you took a philosophy or comparative religion class, and the professor was impressively shrewd and smart He or she had a knack for chopping down the Christian faith of students in the class. It was almost as though the professor delighted in belittling faith in God, and you knew that deep down you weren't educated enough or mentally agile enough to engage in debate. Your faith felt small and ignorant, and doubt crept in. Where do those kinds of sophisticated, superior doubts come from?

Even worse is the kind of doubt you may have seen or lived through that ultimately decides against the Christian faith altogether. It's the kind of doubt that says, "Nope, that's not me anymore. I used to believe a little, but no longer." Maybe you know a friend with those kinds of doubts, which outweigh and overcome faith. Maybe you have had those doubts in the past; maybe you have them right now. Where do they come from? What is the Big Bang of doubt like that? And will locating doubt's Big Bang, in any way, help us stop dwelling in its shadow and move beyond it?

Identifying the source of doubts like this may help us move past them. It turns out that the Bible addresses the source of doubt in an unlikely place: the Book of Psalms. The psalms are hymns and prayers from God's people, who composed, sang, and prayed them over the course of several centuries in ancient Israel and Judah. Some are the songs of individuals, while others are songs of the community; but they all address God with words of praise, thanksgiving, supplication, pain, sadness, anger—the full range of human thought and emotion. The psalms express our words to God; in doing so, they contain a lot of insight into the human experience. And one psalm, Psalm 14, considers a situation in which people live as though God doesn't exist. It has some pretty keen insights into the origin of this kind of attitude and life. What it uncovers as the source of doubt—or at least a source of doubt—might surprise you. Here is Psalm 14, all seven verses:

> 1 Fools say in their hearts, There is no God.
> They are corrupt and do evil things;
> not one of them does anything good.
>
> 2 The LORD looks down from heaven on humans
> to see if anyone is wise,
> to see if anyone seeks God,
> 3 but all of them have turned bad.
> Everyone is corrupt.
> No one does good—
> not even one person!
>
> 4 Are they dumb, all these evildoers,
> devouring my people
> like they are eating bread
> but never calling on the LORD?
>
> 5 Count on it: they will be in utter panic
> because God is with the righteous generation.
> 6 You evildoers may humiliate
> the plans of those who suffer,
> but the LORD is their refuge.
>
> 7 Let Israel's salvation come out of Zion!
> When the LORD changes
> his people's circumstances for the better,
> Jacob will rejoice;
> Israel will celebrate!

Initially, Psalm 14:1 might seem like an odd place to answer our questions about doubt's Big Bang, beginning as it does with more than a little aggression. "Fools say in their hearts, There is no God." It's not exactly friendly to doubts or open to dialogue with doubters. Such a hostile opening may seem more likely to stifle questions than to answer them. But it is deeply reflective of the biblical worldview, which proclaims and worships God as the source of all knowledge and life. Part of bringing doubt out of the shadows and into the light is to recognize that doubting God's existence is fundamentally at odds with what Scripture teaches. We acknowledge and wrestle with our doubts, but we do not celebrate them. From the perspective of biblical wisdom, disbelieving in God's existence—or living as though God doesn't exist—is the apex of arrogance and foolishness.

If the first part of Psalm 14 describes those who deny God's existence, we might anticipate what will come next. We have this image of the super-intellectual doubter in our day and age, the person who confidently believes that there is no such thing as God. We have people such as Richard Dawkins or the late Christopher Hitchens who champion atheism, writing books that forcefully argue against religion. Atheism, as they would have us understand it, is a worldview based on human intelligence, for intellectual people who know better than to believe in superstitious things like an all-powerful being. Given this image of popular atheism in our day, you might have an expectation for what Psalm 14 would say after "Fools say in their hearts, There is no God." We might expect the next line to say one of the following:

They sit in ivory towers and write books.

They hang out with East Coast elites and pontificate at trendy bars and coffee shops.

They corrupt the minds of young collegians.

They studied and weighed all the options carefully and still made the wrong choice.

Truly, in our culture, something like that is the expected description of one who has come to believe in his or her heart that "There is no God." The usual narrative is that someone has *thought* his or her way into believing that God doesn't exist. We're often taught that it's a place your mind can lead you. Doubt seems to come from the human intellect. So that's what we think the next sentence should address in Psalm 14.

Except that's not what comes next in Psalm 14:1. Instead, look at the rest of verse 1: "They are corrupt and do evil things; not one of them does anything good." The psalm goes immediately to *deeds*. Behavior. It considers what people do and how they act. It doesn't say anything about the mind of those who say, "There is no God," but turns right away to a lifestyle of violence and aggression, a life of disobedience that is devoid of goodness. A couple verses later, the psalm becomes incredibly comprehensive in 14:3: "but all of them have turned bad. Everyone is corrupt. No one does good—not even one person!" The psalm starts with a basic denial of God, and in the next few verses it outlines the corrupt way of life that characterizes such an outlook. In the New Testament, Paul quotes Psalm 14:3 in the Book of Romans to make a compelling argument about how sin is ingrained within all of us (Romans 3:9-20). It's where the Christian idea of "original sin" comes from—the notion that sinful desires lie within every human person and only Christ can deliver us from them. Paul points to Psalm 14 as scriptural evidence for widespread evil deeds among humankind.

But in Psalm 14 itself, the logic goes in a different direction. Corrupt deeds are not presented as evidence of humankind's sinfulness; instead, they are held up as the characteristic behavior of those who live as though God doesn't exist. The fools, who say in their hearts, "there is no God," do "evil things," and "not one of them does anything good" (Psalm 14:1). Corrupt actions, the psalm says, go hand-in-hand with disbelief in God. But I don't think it's saying that denial of God leads to corrupt actions. I think it says the reverse: Evil actions lead to denial of God. The fools who deny God might be the beginning of the psalm, but they are the finished product; it's the evil actions, the foolish and corrupt behaviors, that take them down the path toward that destination. What I see in the psalm is that the behavior comes before the doubt. All of the sinful deeds pile one on top of the other, and disobedience and sin multiply until, finally, the one who does these things—the one Psalm 14 calls the fool—decides, "I don't believe in God anymore." When I read Psalm 14, I see doubt's origins in sinful behavior. Disobedience, selfish behavior, sin, and corrupt deeds come first; then doubt follows.

It's very rare that people explore all the options intellectually and objectively and come to a head-only belief that there is no God, or at least one who is remotely interested in what we do. That's usually how we perceive it; but it's not usually how it really goes if we take a close, honest look. People don't typically think their way into doubting; they act their way into doubting. It's much more common that people behave in a certain way; adopt a frankly self-centered mode of living; and then, as if to substantiate it, decide and declare that any God who might possibly disapprove simply does not exist. It's a convenient way to justify and legitimize behavior that stands at odds with the life God calls us to live. ***Doubt justifies disobedience.***

DOUBT JUSTIFIES DISOBEDIENCE.

When you remove God from the equation, you remove accountability to someone or something higher than yourself. In your mind, you remove God so that you can become one, so that you and you alone determine what is acceptable to do or to avoid. This is a pattern that I have noticed in atheists who are famous and in church skeptics who are anonymous. People almost never take an objective, unbiased review of evidence and come to the conclusion that God doesn't exist. It usually starts somewhere else, and it often starts with a pattern or an outlook that becomes deeply settled inside a person, and then doubt takes root as a way to justify what he or she is already doing or desiring to do.

I suppose that this is why I so vividly remember a one-on-one session I had with a man about fifteen years ago now. His frustration was etched in the lines on his face while he vented his feelings about church, faith, Jesus, and God. His emotional vitriol regarding faith was unexpectedly harsh. It was so out of proportion to the questions he was actually asking about it, that I had an insight. So I acted on that insight and asked quietly, "You're getting worked up about faith and church stuff in a way that suggests that something else is really the issue. So is something else going on?"

He stopped. Then his face collapsed. The "something else going on" was a ten-year affair. He had erected the perfect defense against dealing with his infidelity—"I'll just figure out a way not to believe in God anymore." *Doubt justifies disobedience.*

Others may not be involved in a long-term affair, but nevertheless they have other issues manifesting themselves as vehement, out-of-proportion doubt. Perhaps they're contemplating an affair or living in the aftermath of one that just ended. Maybe they want to express anger, either verbally at those they love or digitally at those they hate, and they don't want God to stand in the way. Or maybe it's money, and they want to spend it as they wish and not as some three-thousand-year-old text commands them to. As we've seen so far in this book, some doubts are a natural companion to faith; and we must learn to live with them. We've also seen that some doubts stem from losses that defy measure. But some doubts, if we're honest with ourselves, have their origin in a desire to disobey God and feel at ease about that choice. *Doubt justifies disobedience.*

I harbor anxieties that my point is true not only in individual lives but even in the United Methodist Church of which I am so glad to be a part. As a rule, we Methodists are "nice" and "non-confrontational." But we also have tendencies toward cultural capitulation regarding how we spend our money, how emphatically we declare Jesus, and even on the sensitive issues of sexuality and what we should teach about it. And sometimes I wonder whether in ways large and small we alter our beliefs—"water them down," as some of our more conservative siblings might say—because we have already altered our lives. I fear that we are motivated by convenience as much as by principle. *Doubt justifies disobedience.*

Perhaps you are harboring doubts; perhaps you are even thinking of leaving the faith because of questions you have. Perhaps you have already decided that "there is no God" and you aren't sure why you're even bothering with this book in the first place. If that is the case, I want to ask you a question: What's *really* going on? Be honest with yourself, and ask what it's really all about. Trace your doubt back to its origin, its Big Bang, to see whether it is purely intellectual, or if something else might be nudging you to deny God's existence to allay your conscience. Very few people truly think their way into doubts, innocently arriving at a place of skepticism. You may be one of them. But if not—what's really going on? If you're in the midst of those serious kinds of doubts, I want to challenge you to examine your behaviors, do an honest personal inventory, and acknowledge the possibility that these doubts are self-centered. Make no mistake: This will be difficult. It will require some introspection that might be painful. You may be angry and offended at me for even suggesting it. But often I've found that when we start to doubt God's existence, it's because we're already living as though God doesn't exist. *Doubt justifies disobedience.*

However. Except. But. That is not the end of Psalm 14. Doubt justifying disobedience isn't all of what Psalm 14 has to say; it doesn't stop with those who say in their hearts, "There is no God" because they live accordingly. At the end of the psalm, the focus moves away from the doubters and moves to faithful people. It moves to people who hold on to faith even in the face of their oppressors. Look at 14:6: "You evildoers may humiliate the plans of those who suffer, but the LORD is their refuge." The strong-armed atheists of this psalm don't know that the people who appear weak and humble and pitiful actually

DOUBT JUSTIFIES DISOBEDIENCE, BUT SURRENDER MAGNIFIES UNDERSTANDING.

have God on their side. God is their refuge, and in that refuge is a marvelous combination of strength and clarity. It continues in the next verse: "Let Israel's salvation come out of Zion! When the LORD changes his people's circumstances for the better, Jacob will rejoice; Israel will celebrate!" (14:7). God is a refuge for faithful people, and God will bring about a restoration. There is coming a time, the psalm says, when oppression against believers ceases and faithful people know the source of their deliverance. They see not the Big Bang of their doubt, but the Big Bang of their deliverance. They understand that their deliverance and hope originates with God, and with that knowledge their doubts melt away. And here is what that means: ***Doubt justifies disobedience, but surrender magnifies understanding.***

Surrender to God leads to understanding. Sometimes you've got to *do* in order to *know*. We are called to follow first, and comprehension comes next. We follow the instructions, commands, and teachings without complete clarity, and along the way we discover the reasons why. That's a pattern that we see repeated time and time again in the Bible. God told Abraham to go forth to an unknown land, leaving behind his family, his former life, and all of the emotional and economic security that went along with them. God didn't give him an agenda for the trip, didn't even tell him the destination beforehand. God just sent him "to the land that I will show you," with a promise of greatness. Abraham had to follow without understanding. And so he did (Genesis 12:1-4).

God told Moses to speak to Pharaoh, king of Egypt, and lead the Hebrew people to freedom in the Promised Land (Exodus 3:1–4:17). Moses objected, five times seeking clarification or reassurance from God about what he should do and how he should respond in various scenarios. Moses didn't know about the ten plagues, or the parting of the Red Sea, or the forty years in the wilderness in advance. He had to follow before he fully comprehended what was at stake. He would understand along the way.

Jesus told Peter and his brother Andrew, who were both fishermen, to follow him, with the enigmatic promise that "I'll show you how to fish for people" (Matthew 4:19). Immediately, both brothers left to follow Jesus; and they couldn't have understood very much that early on. I'm sure that Peter had some questions and didn't receive good answers to them right away:

Peter: "Who's keeping the money?"

Jesus: "His name is Judas, and he's got some issues. We'll talk about him later."

Peter: "Who's going to be your right-hand man?"

Jesus: "I think that's going to be you, Peter, and you have some issues. We'll talk about that later."

Peter: "God forbid that you would be crucified!"

Jesus: "Get behind me, Satan."

Peter and the others could not have known what was in store for Jesus or for them. In fact, the Gospels tell us several times about the disciples' frequent lack of understanding. Over and over, the disciples got it wrong as they tried to follow Jesus and comprehend who he was and what he was about. But they followed, nonetheless; and understanding came in time.

The pattern happens throughout the Bible, in both testaments. Those whom God calls follow first and comprehend second. That's the way it works, and it hasn't stopped being true. We surrender to God, obeying at times strange and counter-cultural things, without understanding them. And this Christian way of life, in time, becomes comprehensible as we live into it.

Think of the things we are invited to obey without truly understanding the reason for them. Consider the biblical notion of money management: The Old Testament standard is to give ten percent to God, a tithe (Leviticus 27:30-33). And lest we think we're off the hook because that's the Old Testament and Jesus offers a light, easy burden (Matthew 11:30), we must remember that in the New Testament there was a whole crew of people who gave more than ten percent. They gave and freely shared everything they had (Acts 2:42-47; 4:32-37). Their response to God's grace was to give more, not less, than the prescribed amount. What could more archaic or counter-cultural than the ancient notion of giving ten percent or more to God? It's so tempting to say, "I don't believe in a God who would ask that. Doesn't God know that I've got taxes, alimony, child support, insurance? It can't possibly be relevant today." But understanding comes from obeying God. I hear story after story after story from people at Good Shepherd and elsewhere who have taken the plunge without fully knowing God's rationale or how they will manage it. And in every one of those stories I hear what a blessing it has been for the person or family who committed to following God in this way. They follow first, and comprehension follows. In our own house, my wife and I have been committed to some New Testament levels of giving for years. A few years ago, my wife's company was sold to another company, and all those around Julie lost their jobs. Except her. No reason, no explanation. But God. *Surrender magnifies understanding.*

Or consider the realm of sexual intimacy. Talk about an area where people want to doubt so they can justify behavior! Few things in our culture today are more against the grain than celibacy in singleness and faithfulness in heterosexual marriage. But then, I run across these exceedingly odd yet inordinately blessed couples—young adults and middle aged couples—who wait until marriage to be intimate. And these couples realize that abstinence before marriage reinforces fidelity in marriage. It's the realization that these commands that I thought were cramping my style have ended up saving my life.

THESE COMMANDS THAT CRAMPED MY STYLE ENDED UP SAVING MY LIFE.

The same is true with our relationships: how we express our anger; how we refrain from gossip; how we bless people we could manipulate. Un-Christian behavior toward others has always been a temptation, but it is that much stronger in the digital age when it's so easy to fire terrible comments at other people on the Internet. Just because we think something doesn't mean that we must say it. Just because we hear something juicy doesn't mean that we should pass it on. Just because someone attacks us doesn't mean that we have to respond in kind. Just because we can control others doesn't mean that it is a good thing for us to do so. We show our relational power by restraining it, because in doing so, we imitate Christ. Then God lets us know, through our own experience, that this way of love and care for others works better. *Surrender magnifies understanding.*

Our faith in Jesus Christ is a way of life, and sometimes we have to live it out without comprehending how or why it all holds together. If you're in the middle of a season of doubt, I invite you to surrender yourself to that which you do not fully understand. Follow first, and comprehension will come. Because here's what I truly believe happens when we surrender to that inconvenient, unpredictable, madly-in-love-with-us Savior: We start on a road in the dark, often not seeing more than a step or two ahead. But the longer we walk, follow, and submit, the more clear the ways and will of God become. Doubt justifies disobedience, but surrender magnifies understanding. And when you surrender, you'll experience the Big Bang not of doubt, but of your own living relationship with Jesus Christ.

Questions for Reflection and Discussion

Write responses and other thoughts in the space below each question. If you are discussing the book in a small group, prepare for the meeting by writing answers in advance.

1. Be honest: What are the most compelling reasons you've heard not to believe in God, Jesus, the Bible, or the church? From what sources do you hear that kind of rationale (education, media, study, personal experience, and so forth)?

2. What is the difference between believing that God doesn't exist and living as though God doesn't exist? Which is more common? Which is more tempting for you?

3. Psalm 14:1 seems to be one of the more aggressive verses in the Bible. How do you react to it at first glance?

4. Why does Psalm 14 draw such a close connection between doubt and deeds? Are you surprised by the connection?

5. As you consider doubts you have experienced in yourself and in others, what relationship do you find between doubt and actions? What about between faith and actions?

6. In what ways can doubts be welcome or convenient for you? Does doubt, in any way, justify disobedience in your own life? Why, or why not?

7. The message listed several biblical figures—Abraham, Moses, and Peter—who had to *do* before they *knew*. Which of those characters has a journey with God most like yours?

8. Recall a specific time when you obeyed God before you understood. In that circumstance, did the reasons for God's command and your obedience eventually become clear?

9. Make a list of all of the practices that you do because you are a Christian. These can be individual practices, such as donating money or reading the Bible, or corporate practices, such as worship or baptism. How are these practices expressions of our faith? How have you come to understand your faith more deeply as a result of doing them?

Understand Through Surrender

If you are studying this book in a small group, have each person find a partner. If you have an odd number of participants, one group may be a trio. Have each pair discuss the doubts that they have uncovered or explored during the course of this study. These may include any doubts that led them to try this study or doubts that they have developed since beginning. Allow one partner to give voice to his or her doubts, with the second person listening. The second person should then ask the following questions:

"How is God calling you to surrender in order to understand? How do you feel led to follow Jesus even though you don't fully comprehend everything?"

After the first person has answered these questions, have the second person pray with him or her, asking God to grant understanding and insight through surrender to God's leading. Then switch roles and repeat the process so that the second person may respond. When both partners have shared their doubts, explored God's calling, and prayed for each other, gather the group back together for the closing prayer.

If you are reading this book on your own, try to find a friend to join you for this activity. You may prefer to discuss your doubts and seek guidance from your pastor. Alternatively, you may simply ask the question above to yourself, whisper your response, and pray for God to help you understand God's will.

Closing Prayer

Eternal God, give us courage to surrender to you. Give us the courage and honesty to look inward at our hearts and uncover the source of our doubts, recognizing when they are nothing more than an excuse to stop following you. Whatever the source of our doubt, give us patience and strengthen our faith to follow you without fully comprehending. It is in living a Christian life that we understand the Christian faith. Open our eyes and minds as we continue to look to you. Amen.

Daily Scripture Readings

This week, read the following Scripture passages. Consider how they describe a life of surrender to God.

Monday: Psalm 14:1-7
Tuesday: Romans 3:1-31
Wednesday: Romans 4:1-25
Thursday: Psalm 53:1-6
Friday: Genesis 12:1-20

Other Studies

by Talbot Davis

9781501802881

9781501804311

Order your copies today and continue studying with Davis.

Published by

BKM1566010AR002

SOLVE
FINDING GOD'S SOLUTIONS IN A WORLD OF PROBLEMS
TALBOT DAVIS
Order your copies today and continue studying with Davis.
A NEW STUDY BY
TALBOT DAVIS